HOW TO BUILD YOUR
REPUTATION

How to Build Your Reputation

The Secrets of Becoming the 'Go To' Professional
in a Crowded Marketplace

By Rob Brown

Published by Ecademy Press

HOW TO BUILD YOUR

REPUTATION

BY ROB BROWN

COPYRIGHT © 2007

WWW.THETRIPSYSTEM.COM

Cover Design by **Martin Coote**

Book Design & Typesetting by **Charlotte Mouncey**

Set in *Minion Pro* 12 on 18pt

First published in 2007 by:

Ecademy Press

6 Woodland Rise, Penryn, Cornwall TR10 8QD, UK

info@ecademy-press.com • www.ecademy-press.com

Printed and Bound by:
Lightning Source in the UK and USA

Printed on acid-free paper from managed forests. This book is printed on demand, so no copies will be remaindered or pulped.

ISBN-978-1-905823-11-6

The **TRIP System®** is a registered trademark of Gemarco Ltd

This book is dedicated to two people who don't care how famous, wealthy or good I am, as long as I'm a good father – my incredible daughters, Georgia and Madison.

Acknowledgements

This is my chance to show appreciation for a few special people who can lay claim to helping this book get into your hands...

God Almighty. My rock, my inspiration and my guide. If God is not in your life, you've either got to be really lucky or really good if you want to be a success!

Behind every good man's accomplishments is usually an even better woman who ran his life so he could get on with it! My wife Amanda is that woman. She married a man with a reputation somewhat less than it is now, and she's kept the faith. In doing so, she's kept my feet on the ground while my head was in the clouds!

My TRIP System® team have really helped this project be as good as it is. Kate Kent, my wonderful PA, has organised my schedule, kept me going with words of godly wisdom and painstakingly proofread every word. Andrew Halloway, my Publishing Manager, has read the book 20 times and worked at every stage to get everything perfect. Pierre Dussaucy, my IT Expert, has helped do all the technical things and design the diagrams and tables.

The wider team has been just as influential. My outstanding book coach Mindy Gibbins-Klein was responsible for this being a much better and more authentic book than it ever would have been. Charlotte Mouncey did a beautiful job in laying out the book. Martin Coote's cover design was perfect and the marketing advice from David Petherick was exceptional.

I'm indebted to the friends and mentors who have shaped me along the way and shown me how to build a reputation without even realising it. Richard Nelson, Debra Littler, Dawn, Stuart and Wayne Murry, Peter Williams, David Hill, Glyn Jones, Richard Davies, Alan Brown, Nigel Risner, Paul Emmerson, David Maister, Richard Chaplin, Alistair Kent, Andrew Meadowcroft, Paul Lamb, Mark Gannon, Cindy Gilbert, Marjorie Leonidas, Steve May, Lee Robinson, Roger Galbraith, Norman Kimber, Sir Digby Jones, Mick Fryer, Clive Gott, Paul McGee, Marie Mosely, Shay McConnon, Jeff Monks, Thomas and Penny Power, Will Kintish, Michael Tipper, Simon Hazeldine, Brian Chernett, Graham Jones, Tina Jesson, Eric Carpenter, Graham Davies, Andy Gilbert, Peter Thomson, Andrew Mills, Frank Furness, Mike Southon, John Timperley, Hugh Reynolds and Roger Hamilton.

Thank you for all the things you've done and known it, the wisdom you've acquired and shared it, the ideas you've created and given, and the words of encouragement you've offered and sometimes not been credited for, and the opportunities you've created for me to shine.

Finally, I owe everything to my mother. Strong, funny, merciful, giving, wise and the bearer of great genetics. I've more respect for her than anyone alive. And she still makes the best stews in the world!

So who would you thank in your book? Who's helped make you better than who you might have been if you were doing it alone? More importantly, if I asked a few people in your life who it was that had influenced them in theirs, would they mention your name? After reading and applying the principles in this book, I promise you they will!

How to Get the Most From This Book

Picture the footballer who scores goals with sublime and even impudent skill. They don't know how they do it. They can't analyse it. They just do it. Likewise, some people naturally develop a reputation without any degree of introspection, strategy or process.

For lesser mortals, some kind of reputation manual, instruction book, reliable process, checklist of skills and tasks, roadmap, do's and don'ts, handbook or guide is absolutely vital. Just because you can drive a car doesn't mean you don't need the Highway Code and your Satellite Navigation System.

Whether you realise it or not, you already have a reputation. Problem is, you don't know quite what it is and you don't quite know exactly what you've done to get it. This book will definitely help you. Here are the four ways it could do that:

1. Read **the whole book cover to cover** for a complete grounding in reputation, analysing exactly what yours is, crafting what you'd like it to be, building it systematically and purposefully, and finally keeping it there.

2. Read **Section 1: Understanding Reputations** to get a good feel for what reputation actually is and why it's important to you.

3. Read **Section 2: Designing Reputations** to begin setting your reputation goals and creating the reputation you want through exercises, analysis and application. This

section will also help you get a real handle on exactly what your reputation is and how you got it.

4. Read **Section 3: Building Reputations** for loads of tools, techniques and strategies for building your credibility and your reputation as the 'go to' professional for what you do.

5. Read **Section 4: Defending Reputations** if you know exactly what your reputation is, it's as good as you want it to be and you just want to keep it there.

If you're serious about your reputation, you'll really benefit from the accompanying 140-page **Reputation Building Manual**, which gives you all of the exercises, toolboxes and strategies that you can systematically apply to your situation. Go to www.thetripsystem. com to order your own hard copy or instantly download the e-version. Happy reading and reputation building!

Contents

Foreword *by Sir Digby Jones*

Reputation is now a critical business issue and managing this intangible asset is vital for today's forward-looking individuals and companies.

Reputation is often believed to be uncontrollable because, to some extent, businesses are at the mercy of consumer opinion. But this is a defeatist attitude! As Rob Brown shows in this book, there are many ways to develop your reputation and control this form of 'social capital'.

More than ever, a holistic approach to reputation is essential if this undeniable asset is to be exploited and maintained. In today's market place, there is an increasing emphasis on relationships rather than just presenting offers and winning sales. As such, Rob is in a strong position to educate us about reputation, because of his expertise in relationship marketing as well as reputation building.

I have known many excellent people and businesses that have fallen by the wayside because they didn't pay enough attention to their reputation. By the same token, there are many average companies who could become market leaders if they followed just some of the wisdom in this book.

In this world of time-poor consumers and the vast choice extended to them, those individuals and companies whose reputation precedes them will be the victors.

As the former US Federal Reserve Bank chairman Alan Greenspan said, "In today's world, where ideas are increasingly displacing the physical in the production of economic value, competition for reputation becomes a significant driving force, propelling our economy forward. Manufactured goods often can be evaluated before the completion of a transaction. Service providers, on the other hand, usually can offer only their reputations."

Having spoken at conferences with Rob, I know his dedication and expertise in this largely untouched field will do wonders for your reputation, your wallet and your opportunities.

This book is a 'must read'!

Sir Digby Jones

Former Director-General, CBI

Introduction

First the good news. You already have a reputation. It's either something you purposefully and diligently crafted and marketed to the whole world, or something that evolved by accident because you allowed (whether by accident or design) your clients, customers and contacts to make up their own minds about you.

Second, the bad news. If you allowed it to evolve by itself, then the chances are you don't know exactly what your reputation is, you don't know exactly what you did to get it and you don't know exactly what you need to do to keep it there or change it. Until now!

After reading this book, you'll understand the best way to build your reputation. All you need is the insight and advice I'm going to share with you, and the diligence and discipline to apply yourself to making it work for you.

This book was written for three reasons. First, because I've long been fascinated by how some people become successful and others don't. More importantly, I wondered why some are *perceived* as successful and what part their reputation plays in attracting that success. Now I know.

Second, a book is a great reputation building tool! In the world of non-fiction, unless you're going to be a best-selling writer like my friend Robert Ashton[1], author of 'The Entrepreneur's Book of Lists', the incredible Beermat Entrepreneur Mike Southon[2] or a prolific author like the great adventurer Jonathan Blain[3], you probably won't make millions from your books. But writing a book will give you the same three things it gives me:

1. It raises your profile.
2. It's an excellent marketing tool.
3. It's a fabulous way to share your expertise and knowledge.

Third, the clients I work with, largely in the banking, legal and financial worlds, are demanding. They want to be the advisers of choice, the 'go to' professionals and the stand out option for what they do. To advise them and develop them with integrity, I needed to be doing the same thing myself and also researching it deeply.

I did this by answering five awkward questions about me and my business. Let me ask you the same questions I asked myself. If you can relate to these, you have your hands on the very book with all the answers.

1. Do you want to be more influential, persuasive, credible, respected and rewarded?
2. Are you very good at what you do but find your career and your earnings are not quite fulfilling your potential?
3. Do you struggle to find the clients and customers you really want to work with?
4. Do you find yourself competing on price more often than you would like?
5. Would you like to establish yourself as the obvious expert and the 'go to' professional in your area of expertise?

Did you answer 'yes' to any of these? I ticked yes for all five, which was what started my quest. After reading practically everything ever written on personal branding and the very little there was on building a reputation, I began working what I learned into my life and my business.

> *"It's easy to do what you're doing. It's not so easy to know where you're going."*
> **Simon Woodroffe**, entrepreneur and founder of YO! Sushi

Perhaps like you, I needed to make myself better and 'up my game'. This book has certainly done that! I sometimes call this process *growing a new skin*. This happens when you realise that what has got you to where you are right now is not enough to get you where you want to be in three to five years. That is when you need the new skin that gives you room to grow.

If you want to become an expert, a guru, an in-demand specialist and the 'go to' professional in your field, you have to do four things:

1. **Identify what reputation you have currently**. Although you can get almost anywhere, it might be a longer and different road that takes you there, depending on where you start from.
2. **Decide on the reputation you want.** This will be a blend of your character (what's on the inside), your personal brand (what's on the surface) and your life purpose or long term goals.
3. **Take action to make it happen.** You'll develop a personal

reputation plan, which will probably involve getting really good at something you really enjoy. People respect you for, and pay you to, solve problems. The bigger the problems you solve, the more people will give you the attention, remuneration and recognition you desire. Two of the best ways to learn something and get really good at it is to do it a lot and to teach it to others. That's why I'm going to share with you all the strategies I used to change my income, my circumstances and my opportunities.

4. **Manage your reputation properly**. This is the biggest failure of many professionals today – they do things by accident. Sometimes it's not how good you are that counts, so much as how good others say you are. That's why you'll be learning all the essential personal reputation management techniques available to you!

It doesn't really matter if you are working for someone else in an employed position or you are building your own empire as a sole trader or entrepreneur. You'll find in this book the tools to build your personal reputation strategy using a selection of techniques to suit the person you are, and the skills and strengths you've already got.

Refs

1 Robert Ashton – www.robertashton.co.uk

2 Mike Southon – www.beermat.biz

3 Jonathan Blain – www.jonathanblain.com

Section 1: UNDERSTANDING REPUTATIONS

What Exactly is a Reputation?

Let's begin by properly defining what exactly a reputation is. Your current reputation may be good, bad or indifferent. But you've got one.

If you look up reputation in any good dictionary, you'll find things like this:

1. The general estimation in which a person is held by the public.
2. The state or situation of being held in high esteem.
3. The general opinion of the public towards a person, a group of people or an organisation.
4. Your overall quality or character as seen or judged by people in general.
5. The perception of you and your name in society.

You could say *your reputation is what people say and think and feel about you behind your back.* In other words, when all that's left of you is your business card, what impression do you make? This is my definition:

> *"Your reputation is what influences people to think, feel and talk about you the way they do."*
> **Rob Brown**

A lovely phrase I've coined to describe reputation is **REP** - the **Reason Everyone Pays.** And that's not just financial gain. A good reputation means that people will pay you attention and respect. This is where you may be failing to capitalise - you do not realise that the triple whammy of money, attention and respect are all available if you cultivate a strong reputation.

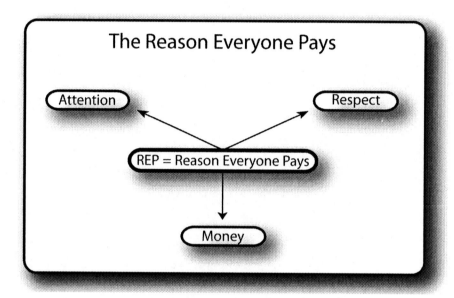

A word about money. Money is good because you can do some great things with more money. You can live a little more abundantly. You can put that money to great use. You can help more people. And you want to be rewarded for your hard work, your knowledge and your expertise! That's money!

> *"It's not what the money makes FOR you, it's what the money makes OF you."*
> **Peter Thomson**[1], leading business guru

A word about respect. Respect is good because there are many maligned experts in the world who are constantly refuted, argued with, rubbished and decried for their knowledge and expertise. But that's not what you want. You want to be spoken of well and recommended often. You want to be held in high regard. You want to be well-thought of and possibly even revered. That's respect!

A word about attention. Attention does not promise you the fame and adoration that comes to celebrities. You probably don't even want that. But you do want a little praise, some sincere appreciation and genuine recognition for your contribution. You do want people to sit up and take notice. That's attention!

If you are not looking for more respect, more attention or more money, then you will lose much of the motivation and desire you need to develop a strong reputation. Andy Gilbert[2], foundational thinker and founder of the Go MAD (Make A Difference) Thinking System, says that unless your 'why' is strong enough, your motivation and action will not be enough to bring about your goal. That means your reputation will come by accident. You'll leave it up to others to decide it for you. You'll be the 'accidental hero' or modest guru. And you'll have little control over what others say, think and feel about everything you are and do.

Many would argue that to be happy and fulfilled, you would want all of these things. When you look at basic human needs, pretty much everyone wants to be *loved and liked* (given time and attention), *acknowledged and treated well* (given respect and recognition) and *remunerated and rewarded* (given the money and resources to do what you want and to live how you want).

Need any more convincing that you need a strong reputation?
Read on!

Who Needs a Strong Reputation?

You may be happy with the reputation you have right now, but I
doubt it, for two reasons. First, if you were happy, you wouldn't
be reading this book. Second, you are, without doubt, a member
of at least one of the following twelve groups, each of whom
need an influential reputation or life, otherwise business may be
a little more uncomfortable than it should be:

**1. Employed professionals looking to move up the corporate
ladder.** This ladder is slippery and already rather crowded with
your peers and colleagues. If you are in danger of being overlooked
for promotion, are not making 'partner' as fast as you would like
or would like to cut your career track to the top a little shorter,
then you need to build a strong reputation.

 *Mark was an associate in a mid-tier law firm. On his
current career track, he was expected to make partner
in another three years. With a wife and two children, he
wanted to shorten this. Through a systematic and carefully
planned reputation campaign, Mark started to raise his
profile inside and outside the firm. With a mixture of
carefully attended and executed networking events, the
choice of a good mentor, some one-to-one coaching and
a series of associations with selected movers and shakers,
Mark achieved his promotion 18 months early.*

2. Anyone looking to make their mark and punch above their weight in a particular field. If you have moved into a new geographical area, a new department, a different business sector or a completely new career, you have a limited time to make an impact. An awareness of the key reputation building tools will radically shorten this 'teething' time and allow you to hit the ground running.

Jocelyn was offered the opportunity to move from London to New York within her international firm of surveyors. She had the triple challenge of a new geographical location, a new role and a brand new team. By adopting two key allies in the New York office ahead of her move, she began to build a reputation for great people skills, a positive attitude and a fun working environment, along with exemplary technical skills. By the time she arrived, a new team was very much on her side. Her job was more to confirm than convince!

3. People placed in positions of trust, authority, management or leadership. Any powerful position where you are given responsibility for people and outcomes will be a test for you. You will be judged by how you influence, motivate and inspire other people to contribute to the future accomplishment of a vision. If you can build a strong reputation, you will significantly increase your chances for respect, buy-in and results.

Lou Gerstner, chairman and CEO of IBM, is a little unusual. Despite most people in his industry wearing jeans and button-down shirts, he almost always appears

in a dark blue suit in photographs. When he took over IBM in 1993, the company was in decline and on the verge of being broken up. Almost everyone expected him to manage the break-up, but Gerstner did not pull the trigger. His reputation in turning round American Express and managing the leveraged buyout of RJR Nabisco meant that he became the first outsider to head this company giant. Although the situation looked bleak, if anyone could turn things around, it was Gerstner. With a move away from the internal focus that had got the company into trouble, his outward-directed, customer-focused ethos ignited the embers and turned the company around.

"*Leadership is action, not position.*"
Donald H McGannon, former CEO of Westinghouse Broadcasting Corporation

4. Entrepreneurs looking to build a company and even an empire around themselves. It is lonely at the top. If you have an entrepreneurial vision, it is likely you will be a lone voice. As somebody famous once said, you have to do it by yourself but you cannot do it alone. By developing the right kind of reputation, you will attract investment, partners, staff, key contacts and all the support and encouragement you need.

 Fred Smith, founder of Federal Express, once famously said that not to be an entrepreneur is to begin the process of decline and decay. People thought he was mad when he

laid down a promise of overnight delivery. On that first night of operations, FedEx delivered 186 packages. Now, with a global workforce of 275,000 people, it is capable of delivering 9.8 million packages in one day. There can be few more successful realisations of an empire built around a vision than this.

5. Self-employed professionals making a living doing what they love to do. Just because you are good at something, doesn't mean you can do it for a living. There are many hungry but talented people out there who do not understand that being successful in the self-employed capacity needs a lot more than talent. You have to be a great marketer, very organised and committed to carving out the right kind of reputation that makes people come to you and minimises your involvement in the things you'd rather not do.

 In Michael Gerber's[3] excellent book, 'The E-Myth - Why Most Small Businesses Don't Work and What to Do About It', he tells the story of Sarah, who loved to bake pies. All she ever wanted to do was bake pies. And it's all she knew how to do. As Gerber chillingly described:

"See the young woman baking pies.

See the young woman start a business baking pies.

See the young woman become an old woman."

Throughout the book, Gerber shows Sarah how to put the systems in place so that she worked on the business and not in it. Part of working on your business is doing the marketing and reputation building that makes everything else a whole lot easier.

6. Visionaries who want to grow something big and meaningful, and leave a legacy long after they have gone. Some people say that your character is what you have when you arrive in a new town and your reputation is what you have when you leave. You can control what people think and say about you, if you give them the right cues. But to build an empire, you need to have a very strong character. In fact, it is impossible to develop a strong reputation without a correspondingly strong character. Only when you develop yourself can you build something bigger than you are.

 Walter Disney was born in Chicago in 1901 and spent his early years on a 45-acre farm in Madeline, Missouri. Then his family moved to Kansas City, where he grew up. In 1918, he dropped out of high school and left to join the Red Cross ambulance corps. He arrived in post-war France and spent a year as a chauffeur for Army officers. He returned to Kansas City in 1919 and spent a couple of years doing odd jobs. But then he got interested in animation and was so taken by it that he founded a company in 1922 to produce cartoons full time. He had a series of setbacks, but didn't give up. He went to California and started a cartoon company in 1923 with his brother Roy. The rest is history. As he famously said, "All our dreams can come true, if we have the courage to pursue them." This man had the courage and the vision to build something he believed would live long after he had gone. "I would rather entertain and hope that people learned something than educate people and hope they were entertained."

> *"Life is for one generation, a good name is forever."*
> **Japanese proverb**

7. Anyone thinking of starting their own company or business venture. If people are going to buy you or buy from you, they need to be able to trust you. They want to know that you can do what you say you will do, when you say you will do it. They need to know you are a safe pair of hands. They need to know they are getting value.

Your reputation is more about you than your company. Getting known by the right people for the right things will help you attract all the customers and clients you need to make your business successful.

> *"To be trusted is a greater compliment than to be loved."*
> **George MacDonald,** Scottish author, poet and
> Christian minister (1824 – 1905)

 Gordon planned to leave corporate life in the interests of work-life balance. He looked at many alternatives, and finally decided to go into life coaching. He gave himself two years in which to reach 70% of his corporate income. But because of a clever programme of networking, article writing and freelance coaching in the last nine months of his job, Gordon had six clients in place on the day he left. In the space of a year, he was able to build up enough business to reach his target. This is a classic example of building a reputation you will need for the future.

8. People who want more recognition, reward and acknowledgement for who they are and what they do. Above pay and working conditions, you would probably cite appreciation as one of the key motivators in your job. Unfortunately, if you are like most people, appreciation will be in short supply. These days, it is not enough to do a good job. If you want to be more loved and appreciated, you have to be perceived as doing a good job by the right people at the right time. If you want more respect for what you are doing, you cannot leave this to chance. There are things you can do to get noticed and thanked. But you must take responsibility and take action, as it will not happen by accident.

> *"Do not worry about holding high position; worry rather about playing your proper role."*
> **Anon**

 Sue was a good event organiser. She sourced great venues for clients and helped co-ordinate several successful events. However, aside from a few people saying 'thank you', Sue felt she was never really winning the accolades her events deserved. The problem was that all of her competitors were doing the same good job. She decided to take a different direction. She began offering clients a follow-up and feedback service. This involved audio and video testimonials from delegates and guests, as well as interviews with key speakers, venue staff and even the audiovisual crew. Once the clients began to see what a great buzz had been created and what value Sue was offering, they began to invite her to planning and strategy meetings for future events. This was the recognition she was yearning for.

9. Professionals fed up with a lack of appreciation from their peers. Sometimes you find that your clients and customers rate you, but your colleagues and team cannot muster the same enthusiasm for your work. This is often a matter of ignorance. Don't 'hide your light under a bushel'. It is no good you being the best kept secret in the world. You must raise your profile purposefully and deliberately if you want to be known and appreciated more than you are.

Nicky worked in a large consulting firm. She had a great relationship with her clients, but couldn't seem to generate a similar level of admiration amongst her peers. As a result of external coaching, she realised that her profile within the firm was too low. By volunteering for a series of projects, sitting on and eventually running a sub-committee and finally building a social relationship with one of the partners, she became one of the most respected and well-known people in her region. It took twelve months.

10. Professionals who want to charge premium rates for their excellent advice, and are tired of haggling and competing on price. You must remember that price is only ever an objection in the absence of value. If people are arguing about price, they cannot see the value that you bring to the table. You must educate them on what you do differently and beyond your competitors. In doing so, you give clients more of a reason to choose you and less of a reason to undermine their investment in what you offer. Your reputation can help you do this.

> *"Credibility is being believed and trusted by your customers and potential customers. You can't buy it. No amount of advertising or promotion can hand it to you on a platter."*
> **Anon**

 Ron was a project management consultant working in notoriously tight public sector markets. Fed up with being squeezed by hard negotiating procurement departments, Ron began to rethink his approach. By undertaking a joint survey with one particular client, he showed that lessons from previous projects had not been internalised and departments had wasted significant sums of money repeating similar mistakes. By moving to a results-based 'per project' rather than 'per day' rate, Ron began offering longer-term development packages to underpin the project work he was already doing. This equated to a higher day rate, which the client was happy to pay since the outcome was not short-term impact but more long-term, sustainable change.

11. Professionals who want to attract a certain type and quality of client but seem to be in a position where they must take every client that comes their way. Whether you realise it or not, you have more than one reputation for more than one thing. For example, your family will see you in a different way to your clients. Your job is to make sure the right people see you in the right way, and to do the right things as a result. If you can define your target audience, you can go after them, market to them and position yourself in front of them. This way, when people need what you do, they come to you first.

Andrew was an average accountant in an average, mid-size firm, working in an average tax department. He wanted more, and he realised that if he continued to do all the things he was doing, progress would be painfully slow. Not a natural marketer, Andrew decided that average abilities as an accountant need not hold him back in his career. He embarked on a reputation-building programme revolving around expertise and timing. Through a series of special reports and radio appearances at key financial moments, he developed a reputation as a tax expert on budget and interest issues. Clients began approaching the firm asking for him by name. Business has never been the same since!

> *"Never become so much of an expert that you stop gaining expertise. View life as a continuous learning experience."*
> **Denis Waitley,** best-selling author of 'The Seeds of Greatness' and 'The Psychology of Winning'

12. People who want business to be easier, more fun and more lucrative! Most business professionals are not natural salespeople. Like them, you are probably excellent at what you do, and very technically competent. Unfortunately, part of your role will be to win new business and create new opportunities. For many people, this can take the fun out of what you love doing, and if you are failing in this area it can also adversely affect bonuses and promotion prospects.

Mark had been in banking for 25 years. Moving up through the retail and commercial departments, he was now a

corporate relationship manager, dealing with businesses turning over £2 million plus. He had become increasingly resentful of the time he was forced to spend networking and cold calling, when he simply wanted to look after his existing clients. After some mentoring intervention, Mark realised that while his reputation was good amongst his existing clients, he was not leveraging this to win more business. With help, he put together a programme of testimonial gathering, referral marketing and third-party endorsements which enabled him to hit his annual new business targets within nine months.

If you fit into one or more of these categories, then you can either continue doing what you've been doing and hope that you turn a corner, or you can build a **Personal Reputation Plan** (PRP). This book will help you create the most pro-active plan that's right for you and your circumstances!

Why YOU Need a Strong Reputation

The short answer is that a bad reputation will kill you! You'll struggle in business, and this will adversely affect your personal life. You'll take on roles and jobs because you have to, not because you want to. You'll find yourself in the despicable position of fulfilling other people's dreams and achieving other people's goals.

As you've learned, you get paid for solving problems. And the bigger the problems, the more you tend to get paid. But you need to position yourself so you can be considered and then engaged to solve those problems, otherwise you go hungry. You need to be sought after and 'front of mind' if you're even going to get a chance to solve people's problems.

It doesn't matter if you're the best person to do the job. From my experience, the best opportunities, clients and customers do not always fall to the best professionals, the best at networking, the best salespeople or the best rainmakers. They fall to those who have the strongest reputation in the marketplace. They fall to those with the greatest 'top of mind' awareness. They fall to those who have a personal reputation which makes them the obvious expert and the 'go to' professional for what they do. Is that you?

Please understand this. *It's not enough to be the best. You have to be seen to be the best.* The plain truth is that you need a proper strategy to create a credible and desirable reputation, and the action plan to lift it into the minds of your target audience. That way, when they need what you do, they think of you first, above and beyond all of their other choices.

The Ten Universal Laws of 21ˢᵗ Century Business

There is no way round it. You need a reputation to be truly successful in business these days. It is increasingly a critical issue. A simple mistake or misunderstanding can wipe out a reputation in one blow, or at the least, seriously damage it.

> *"Reputation is a vital form of capital,*
> *as vital as money is a form of actual capital."*
> **Angus Matthew**[4], relationship marketer

So there is an ongoing need to assess all your activities, to ensure they all contribute to your reputation rather than undermine it. Consider a company's reputation. It depends on the perceptions and experiences of all its stakeholders: employees, customers, shareholders, suppliers, partners – even government bodies, the media and analysts. In fact, anyone who relates to it as a brand. You are no different as an individual. Who are your stakeholders, and how are they perceiving you?

In our information technology age, rumours can spread round the world in an instant. Negative information promoted on the web can be very difficult to overcome. Pressure groups and campaigners have forced even the biggest of multi-national companies to change policies in order to preserve their reputation. Sometimes these decisions to cave in to pressure have been taken even when the complaint is unjustified – for the sake of preserving reputation.

 When Shell wanted to scupper the Brent Spar oil platform at sea in the early 1990s, there were howls of protest from environmentalists. In 1995, Greenpeace occupied the platform, and the oil company was forced to change its mind. Many customers had boycotted Shell products, losing Shell millions of dollars. Shell took the expensive option of clean-up and recycling the whole structure rather than risk reputation damage, even though the protesters were mis-informed. Apparently the destruction of the platform would not have caused as much pollution as it was claimed.

The *proliferation of choice* and the *time-poor lifestyles* of people today mean that competing for consumer attention is getting harder and harder. Developing your reputation can help you rise above that. If you are the first to come to mind, the customer may not go anywhere else.

There is also another emerging factor: an increasing expectation that business should act as a positive agent for social change. It's no use crying, "We're a business, not a charity!" anymore. If you are not seen as a positive contributor to society, you are at a competitive disadvantage. Perhaps because people have lost trust in politicians and the government's ability to change the world, they are seeing businesses as agents of change. It even has a name – **Corporate Social Responsibility.** And it has powerful potential for reputation-building, provided it is demonstrably seen as genuine, rather than yet another business gimmick.

A high reputation is also significant in attracting high calibre employees, and motivating the ones you have. Suppliers also offer better deals to those companies they perceive to have a top reputation – simply hoping that some of it will rub off on them. They love the association, and are prepared to negotiate to get some of it!

In short, **REPUTATION** represents the best way to succeed in today's business world. To fully understand how you can build yours, you need to know what you're up against. In the last 20 years, **Ten Universal Laws of 21st Century Business** have skewed the commercial landscape.

If you want to position yourself as the number one provider/ supplier/adviser of choice, you'll need to be either very lucky and do it by accident, or really clever and do it on purpose. So let's look at these laws in detail.

The Ten Laws of 21st Century Business

R elationship Deterioration

E xponential Expectations

P redatory Competition

U nprecedented Opportunity

T echnological Advancement

A ggressive Pricing

T rust Erosion

I nformation Overload

O verloaded Resources

N iche Proliferation

1. Relationship Deterioration

In 2005, I coined a phrase to explain why relationships are becoming more and more strained, and therefore more and more vital in business success. I called it *The Law of One Step Removed*. You know how, these days, you meet someone for a quick coffee when you should meet them for a longer lunch? You phone someone when you should meet them? You e-mail or write to someone when you should phone them? You text someone when you should e-mail them? This puts relationships at a premium, both in the personal and business domain. Companies that claim to be client focused or put the customer first, seem to conveniently substitute 'profits first'. Relationships are central to reputation, as you will learn later.

2. Exponential Expectations

You may have heard the phrase that 'yesterday's great is tomorrow's average'. What was brilliant in the past now seems ordinary for today's consumers. In this age of customer/client experience, more and more companies look to 'wow' and 'delight', which pushes the bar of expectations ever higher. Of course, every nudge of the bar has a cost implication that ultimately affects profitability.

3. Predatory Competition

If your competition was merely healthy and played by ethical rules on a level playing field, you *may* be able to compete. Unfortunately, your rivals actively chase your customers and clients, who are lured, poached, coerced, bullied, flattered and romanced on a daily basis. So while your back is turned to look for your own 'new chickens', the fox comes in and steals those you already have.

The marketing director of one of the world's leading telecoms companies was being interviewed on UK radio. He was asked, "What are your business goals for the next twelve months?" He replied, "To win two million more customers." The interviewer laughed, saying, "Surely you know that everyone who wants a mobile phone has got one by now?" The director answered simply, "Yeah, we know that. We want everyone else's customers."

4. Unprecedented Opportunity

There are now around nine million people in the world with $1m or more in the bank. This is growing every day, from the ranks of both the employed and the self-employed. With lowered barriers to market and decreased job security, the entrepreneurial boom means more and more people are going into business for themselves. There are more ways to make money and more people to give it to you than at any other time. Unfortunately, this money does not flow into the pockets of those who are merely competent. To stand a chance of competing, you have to be good at what you do AND be good at marketing what you do.

5. Technological Advancement

There is no doubt that technology is king, with a wealth of unbelievable innovations that can give you the edge if you use them right. Unfortunately, this has two negative spin-offs for you in today's world of business. First, technology is changing the way you work. Whether that comes through globalisation of markets or the outsourcing of your skills to machines, you could one day be made obsolete. Second, it makes for more discerning prospects. People can use technology to find out anything they need to know, and fast. They can easily find someone else to do what you do, or even source the technology and knowledge to do it themselves! Your reputation could give them a reason to come to you.

6. Aggressive Pricing

In the drive for shareholder value and profitability, it is easy to get caught up in the battle to cut your costs and decrease spending on one side, while increasing your turnover and sales on the other. This has inevitably led to more and more commoditising of both products and services. As more discerning buyers insist on 'more for less', businesses across all sectors are being forced to compete on price. This has an adverse effect on service levels, which in turn leads to less attractive value propositions for customers and clients. There is only one way to cut through this problem – build a reputation for adding value and for being worth it!

7. Trust Erosion

People are losing faith in the government, in the judicial system, in the armed forces and police, in public services and in businesses. Trust is being eroded in neighbours, communities and relationships. Divorce is at an all-time high. Relationship breakdown is at an all-time high.

> *"Without trust there is nothing."*
> **Anon**

Loyalty is at an all-time low. Professional athletes seem to switch sports teams on a whim, while in the boardroom, money often shouts louder than morals. Job security is a thing of the past -

the average 45-year-old has had more than twelve jobs so far in their lifetime. If your reputation fosters trust in your business, your dealings and your relationships, you stand a strong chance of differentiating yourself from the crowd.

 A huge crowd was watching the famous tightrope walker, Charles Blondin, cross Niagara Falls one day in 1860. He crossed it numerous times – a 1,000 foot trip 160 feet above the raging waters. He not only walked across it, he also pushed a wheelbarrow across it. One little boy just stared in amazement. So, after completing a crossing, Blondin looked at that little boy and said, "Do you believe I could take a person across in the wheelbarrow without falling?" "Yes, sir, I really do," came the reply. Blondin said, "Well then, get in, son." Believing is one thing. Trusting is another. What are you doing to make people step into your wheelbarrow?

8. Information Overload

Multi-channel television and radio, digital technology, wireless communications and the monster that is the internet all mean that you can now get what you want, when you want it, almost instantaneously. On the downside, this means everyone is busy and everyone is cluttered. Getting your message home to prospective buyers and users is a harder and harder sell. With the average man in the street being subjected to thousands of advertising messages every day, the chances of making enough of a mark to induce a buying decision is ever more remote and costly. Cutting through the clutter without a huge advertising budget is almost impossible without a strong reputation.

9. Overloaded Resources

Where does all your time go? Where does all your energy go? Your role has changed over the last few years. Instead of just being a technically accomplished professional, you have to be able to market and sell what you do. You are given business development targets. You are made to network, attend business functions, generate new accounts and create more opportunities. Time overload and role overload put pressure on your performance and your personal relationships. And this is going to get worse. There must be smarter ways to work and cleverer ways to market what you do. Guess what? There is. It's through your reputation!

10. Niche Proliferation

The age of the specialist is here. There are whole law firms who specialise in just one discipline, such as intellectual property, or international litigation. Some accountancy firms focus solely on tax work or forensic accounting. There are now banking professionals who concentrate solely on property or retail. Many life coaches only work with a segment of the market such as dentists, or divorced women. Thousands of consultants cater purely for the public sector. Make no mistake – the age of the generalist has gone. You must consider niching to survive. You will learn later how to craft your reputation as a niched specialist.

All of the **Ten Universal Laws of 21st Century Business** outlined above *can* be broken or ignored. But you will be missing many chances to compete if you do so. It is far better to make these laws work for you. They can be your friend, if you can develop the one thing that will cut through them all to bring you the maximum profits, opportunities, enjoyment and success – **REPUTATION.**

> *"You can't build a reputation on what you're going to do."*
> **Henry Ford**, pioneering US vehicle manufacturer (1863-1947)

Now you know exactly what reputation means, and why you need a good one, let's look at the benefits a good reputation is going to bring you.

What a Good Reputation Will Do for You

Some people develop a good reputation by accident. Some people develop a good reputation by doing a good job and hoping it will come to them. And some people develop a good reputation by strategically and systematically deciding what they want to be known for and creating that perception accordingly. Why go to that trouble? Because it's worth it!

But whichever way you come by it, there are **ten positive outcomes of a powerful reputation in business**. All these outcomes are things that may happen naturally and organically, but over a long period of time. If you make the effort to purposely build your reputation, it allows you to access these benefits much more quickly.

In becoming known as the 'go to' professional for what you do, a great reputation...

1. Helps You Avoid Feast and Famine Cycles

Many employed and self-employed professionals experience the intense activity of business delivery, only to find that their marketing suffered during those hectic times, and their pipeline is rather empty. 'Good days, bad days' can turn into 'good months, bad months'. If you deal in large corporate accounts, it can even mean good years, bad years. Many of my banking clients are fed up of making their targets on a 'lucky deal' and now prefer to make it happen *on purpose*. Being known by the right people for the right reasons means that you position yourself so strongly that you do not need to go out and market yourself so much. In other words, people come to you instead of you going to them.

2. Makes You Stand Out From the Crowd

> *"This is the age of the surplus society, where too many companies employ too many similar professionals, with similar qualifications and experience, for similar wages, to deliver similar products and services to similar clients and customers for similar prices and similar results."*
>
> **Rob Brown**

Think carefully about how you're going to stand out. If you are predictable, it can sometimes mean you are not memorable. Which is another way of saying you are history and you are forgotten. When somebody needs what you do, you want them to think of you first, above and beyond all of their other choices. This is why you need to differentiate, and a strong reputation allows you to do just that.

If you are looking for a way to decrease your reliance on cold calling, paid for advertising and other traditional marketing methods, a strong reputation should be your chief weapon. It has been said that the strategy for business survival is visibility. Taking this one step further, the strategy for business success is focused, enhanced visibility in the right markets at the right time.

When you differentiate, you give people a reason to choose *you* instead of *everyone else*. It makes you not just a professional, but *the professional of choice*. Not just a business, but *the business everyone wants to work with*. This is not just so that people know you as the obvious expert but that they also come to you and make the decision to use you.

If what you do has competitors of any kind, then all of your prospects can choose not to use you and go somewhere else. If what you do is optional, then your prospects can choose not to use you or anyone else. Either way, you need a strong reputation to carve out a lane along which the people who need you, can both see you and get to you quickly. If you have a clear and distinct reputation, then it's easier for people to clearly see their need for you.

> "*If what you do is optional or has competitors, you must give people a strong reason to choose you. That's what a reputation does!*"
>
> **Rob Brown**

3. Helps You Compensate for Poor Marketing

You may be brilliant at what you do. You could even be a world beater. But unless enough people are willing to pay you enough money for what you do or sell, you will never make your business a success. *It's no good being the best kept secret in the world.* These days, everyone is in the marketing business.

If you are poor at educating your target market about the wonderful things that you do, you will always struggle to attract the business and revenues you need. You may lack the ability or the inclination to market, and this is normal. Not everyone is blessed with either a marketing mind or a marketing motivation. Still, the result is the same - no business and no revenue. By developing a strong reputation, you position yourself so that people come to you instead of you having to go to them. It takes the effort out of marketing!

4. Buys You More Time

The average business professional works a 50-hour week and a 48-week year. By any standards, this is a brutal regime. You do not do it because you want to, but because you have to. Perhaps you are employed, and are set targets for activity, chargeable hours and business development. Or you could be self-employed, which essentially means that if you do not work, you do not eat. Either way, probably 25-50% of your working week is spent on marketing what you do (and the associated administration that goes with that). This is largely undertaken with varying degrees of commitment and success. A strong reputation helps you become the provider or adviser of choice. This saves you an enormous amount of time and stress.

5. Helps You Create More Opportunities

Everyone wants the opportunity to work with interesting clients on challenging and enjoyable projects. And everyone wants to feel their work opens doors rather then closes them.

If you are in an employed situation, then increasing your worth to the company will bring you more career options, promotions, pay-rises, perks and equity options. It will probably also bring you interest from other companies and head-hunters.

If you sail your own ship, you will come across more interesting and lucrative projects, joint ventures, alliances and contracts. It will show you different directions, alternative marketing channels and open up multiple income sources.

Whatever your employment situation, a strong reputation puts you 'in the game'. That means you get the opportunity for pitches, proposals and tenders that you would never have had before. That means more follow-up work and repeat business that may not have come your way. That means the chance for more referral business. That means the chance to work with the kind of people you like working with. That means the choice to work **OR NOT.**

6. Increases Your Security

An added bonus of creating a strong reputation is long-term survival. It safeguards your job/role in tough economic times. There are no jobs for life. You may not even want a job for life. But you do want the choice. Good people always have options regardless of the economic or industry climate.

7. Gains You More Preferential Treatment

This comes in the form of recognition and appreciation. As well as more favourable publicity and desirability, your strong reputation will bring you more approval, thanks and gratitude. This will come in the form of rewards, compliments, awards and opportunities.

A strong reputation makes you more memorable and likely to be chosen ahead of your competitors. This brings you a certain exclusivity, celebrity and even fame, which allows you to dictate who you work with and for. You also earn the right to say how you work by dictating the rules of engagement.

8. Increases Your Influence

Many of my clients cite this as the biggest reason they want to develop their reputation. Perhaps this is because, when you become more influential, pretty much all of these other benefits click into place.

When you increase your influence, you increase your reach. You begin touching people's lives and you make a difference. This is not only while you are there, but long after you have gone. You start to affect behaviour, and change the way people think and feel. This brings with it enormous responsibility and also huge rewards.

Like a pebble that makes ripples in a pond, a strong reputation means that you are known in wider and wider circles. Your reach is both powerful and extended, creating more opportunities to build an empire, leave a legacy and make a difference.

A powerful reputation increases your credibility and trust both internally, if you are employed, and externally in the marketplace. It enhances your authority and respect as a leader, which makes it easier for you to motivate, persuade and inspire those around you. It also attracts other influential people to you, such as advisers, mentors, experts, strategic partners, key decision-makers and even choice employees and team members.

9. Makes More Money and Profits

Let's not deny it – money is important. As Zig Ziglar said, '*It ranks right up there with oxygen!*' When I founded the **TRIP System®**, I had one eye on building wealth for myself AND my clients. That's what **Turning Relationships into Profits** is all about, and your reputation is a key part of that strategy.

By attracting the right kind of customers/clients and more of them, your business will become more profitable and more successful. A strong reputation wins you higher value work and increases your earning potential through fees, bonuses and commissions. It 'ups your game' and allows you to dine at different tables with different people. Ultimately it helps you win more lucrative work. And who doesn't want to earn more for working less with more interesting clients and customers?

10. Lets You Have More Fun!

Life is much more satisfying when you have the time and money to do what you want with it. And work is much more enjoyable when warm, qualified prospects come to you instead of you having to go after them. It's an easier life when you have the space and choice to either *work or not*. It's wonderful when you have the freedom to choose the people you want to work with.

Peter Jackson, director of the fabulously successful 'Lord of the Rings' film trilogy, famously relates that a key factor in his casting decisions was choosing the actors he felt he could get along with over an extended period of filming. In the same way, you will find work more enjoyable when you can pick who you want to work with, and you will attract more business yourself if you are fun and easy to get along with.

You live in an era where low job satisfaction is a contributory stress factor. Recent surveys show that more than half of people would change their job tomorrow if they could get the job they wanted. Work/life balance is eroded with long working weeks and years and the extra pressure of targets and performance-related pay. When you create a strong reputation, you'll find that these kinds of things become less of an issue as the excitement and enjoyment come back into your life, and business becomes fun again.

What a Reputation Probably Won't Do for You

You may now be thinking that building a strong reputation is the answer to all of your problems. Well, not quite! Creating a great reputation is essential, but it can't do everything for you. Here are a few things it probably won't accomplish:

- Make you a household name or make you famous by itself
- Turn you into an overnight success
- Cover up any incompetence, lack of professionalism or poor quality in your work
- Hide your weaknesses and your insecurity
- Achieve all of your goals and dreams
- Overcome a lack of integrity

> *"Real integrity is doing the right thing, [despite] knowing that nobody's going to know whether you did it or not."*
> **Oprah Winfrey**, chat-show host
> (in 'Good Housekeeping')

Making a Quantum Leap

So what now?

If you want to avoid the feast and famine cycle, the insanity of sameness and the claustrophobia of clutter... **If** you want to compensate for a lack in marketing and buy more time... **If** you want to create more satisfaction and enjoyment, more preferential treatment, more opportunities, a differentiated market position, more influence, more money and more profits...

Then you need to make changes, take action and read on! Whether you are employed or self-employed, some or all of these benefits are available to you, but you're not going to attain them by just doing all the things you've already been doing.

What has got you to where you are today will at best maintain your current position over the next three to five years. If you want to make quantum leaps and major steps towards the success you desire, you need a different plan and a better plan. Your reputation is the most powerful asset you have in making this difference. Here's why...

Why Your Reputation is Your Most Valuable Asset

Your reputation is in many ways the most valuable thing you own. It can take years to build and be destroyed in an instant.

> *"A reputation once broken may possibly be repaired, but the world will always keep their eyes on the spot where the crack was."*
> **Joseph Hall**, English bishop and satirist (1574-1656)

You only need to look at the PR gaffes and howlers throughout history to see how fragile a reputation can be. This is especially so when the 'brand' is a person rather than a company.

 Famous jewellery mogul Gerald Ratner cut his teeth selling in London's Petticoat Lane Market as a boy. He learned quickly that "the people who shouted the loudest and appeared to give the best offers sold the most." This idea of shouting loud was to be his undoing later! He joined the family business in 1966, and built up an extremely successful chain of jewellers during the 1980s, of which he became Chief Executive. The shops shocked the formerly staid jewellery industry by displaying fluorescent orange posters advertising cut-price bargains, and by offering low price ranges.

Although widely regarded as 'tacky', the shops and their wares were nevertheless extremely popular with the public, until Ratner made a speech at the Institute of Directors in April 1991. During the speech, he said: "We also do cut-glass sherry decanters complete with six glasses on a silver-plated tray that your butler can serve you drinks on, all for £4.95. People say, 'How can you sell this for such a low price?' I say, because it's total crap."

He compounded this by going on to remark that some of the earrings were "cheaper than an M&S prawn sandwich but probably wouldn't last as long."

The speech was instantly seized upon by the media and

an estimated £500m was wiped from the value of the company. He was sacked 18 months later, and in 1994 the Ratner name was expunged from the company, to be renamed Signet Group.

Even today, the British retail industry uses the term 'doing a Ratner' to describe a PR debacle that destroys a reputation. Although Ratner has said in his defence that it was a private function which he did not expect to be reported, and that his remarks were not made seriously, it is clear his reputation was decimated by his loud mouth!

Here's why your reputation is more valuable than…

Your Skills

These were often thought of as your strongest asset, but not anymore. In the age of specialists, *all skills can now be acquired, outsourced or bought.* This is why so many people are going into business for themselves - to provide specific skills for all kinds of businesses and situations.

This is the age of experts and 'nichers' - people who excel in a particular field. Instead of heart surgeons, there are now surgeons who specialise in a certain kind of heart operation, or a specific area of the heart. With very few exceptions, no matter how good you are at a particular facet of your role, there will always be somebody who does that day in and day out. It's all they do and they're brilliant at it! This is because whatever you do a lot of, you get really good at. And they're available for hire!

Your skills can be replicated and replaced. While certain skills will add to your reputation, it is dangerous to build a reputation just on being skilful. Your skills can be switched and transferred. Your reputation cannot.

Your Knowledge

Tim Kidson and Sharon Niccoll, authors of 'Pilgrim's Progress: How to be a WINNER in the Global Knowledge Economy', state that **knowledge takes two forms – *explicit* and *tacit*.** Explicit knowledge is in the public domain. It's accessible, widely available (if you know where to find it) and rarely provides a competitive edge, even if it is specialised. Because people can access it and often know where to find it, they are less likely to come to you and pay you to give it to them.

Tacit knowledge is more unique. It's what resides in your head. It's made up of your experience, your intelligence, your personality, your behaviour. It is more about 'knowing how' than just 'knowing'. In this respect, it is much more valuable. Clearly nobody is wired quite like you, and nobody knows the exact blend of knowledge that you know. It is also clear that your tacit knowledge can bolster your reputation. But you can still see how this kind of stuff can also be bought, outsourced, sub-contracted, acquired and hired. If not, then the vast army of consultants, mentors and advisers in the world would be out of a job!

Your Experience

Endurance athletes call this 'miles in the bank'. If you've been round the block, earned a few grey hairs, been through a lot of

53

change, managed some tough situations, overcome adversity and accomplished great things, then you start to generate experience. They say you cannot buy experience, but there are now many experts, millionaires, entrepreneurs, business leaders and young companies doing exactly that. They haven't got the experience themselves, but by shrewd use of networks, advisers and mentors, they are able to bring in the experience they need to build the reputation they want.

Your Client List

Your database might be considered to be your greatest asset, but not always. Without a good reputation, even the biggest and most prestigious client list in the world wouldn't buy from you. Moreover, you can always get another list. Essentially, a client list is simply a list of names. If you had to re-start your business from nothing tomorrow, you can buy lists of names with any biographical and demographical profile. You can also build and acquire such lists. Alas, you can rarely regain a reputation because it is usually carved out over a long period of time and yet can be shattered in an instant.

> *"Greatness is not found in possessions, power, position, or prestige. It is discovered in goodness, humility, service, and character."*
> **William Arthur Ward**, author of 'Fountains of Faith' and one of America's most quoted writers of inspirational maxims (1921–1994)

So where does this leave you? Your client list, your skills, your experience and your knowledge can (to some extent) be duplicated and substituted. But your reputation cannot. It doesn't matter how much you know, how much you have or how much you've lived. That stuff only becomes useful and valuable to someone if they know about you. And only then can you begin to make your reputation count.

> *"The best way to benefit from a good reputation is just to keep doing the things that earned it for you in the first place. That's not a bad way to lead a life, or run a business."*
> **Anon**

Now that you have seen what a reputation is, why you need a good one and what it will do for you in your business, it is time to unpack exactly how you can exploit the power of reputation.

The first step is to be clear about the difference between character, personal brand and reputation. Many people become confused about this – but you needn't anymore. Read on!

The Difference Between Character, Personal Brand and Reputation

Your inner 'character' is integral to what comes out in your branding and reputation. For example, if truthfulness is something that comes naturally to you, it will surface in your reputation. But if being truthful is not part of your core personal values, it will be very much harder to create a reputation for truthfulness in your work. By aligning your inner character and values to your outer personal brand, you can begin designing and controlling the reputation you desire.

> *"Be more aware of your character than your reputation.*
> *Your character is who you are; your reputation is merely*
> *what other people think you are."*
> **Anon**

The simple diagram below shows the relationship between your inner personality (often defined as the combination of emotional, intellectual and moral qualities that distinguishes an individual), your outward brand and your wider reputation.

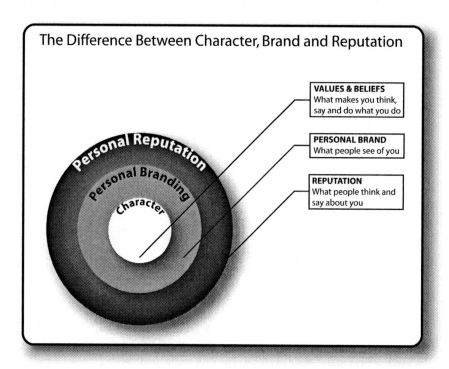

The Difference Between Character, Brand and Reputation

VALUES & BELIEFS
What makes you think, say and do what you do

PERSONAL BRAND
What people see of you

REPUTATION
What people think and say about you

Personal Reputation
Personal Branding
Character

The table opposite will help you unpack in more detail the difference between these three elements.

Character	Personal Brand	Reputation
Internal moral and mental construction and wiring	External manifestation and image	Interpretation by others
Inside	Surface	Outside
Qualities you can't easily fake	Attributes you can influence and shape	Perceptions you can control
What you see	What other people see and hear	What other people think, say, feel and do as a result
What you remember	What you want people to remember	What people remember
What makes you speak the way you do	What people think while you're speaking	What people think before and after you speak
Revealed by circumstances	Influenced by circumstances and character	Influenced by personal brand, character and circumstances
Who you are	Who you want to be	Who others think you are
The real face	The photograph	The reaction to the photograph
Measured inwardly by peace of mind, happiness and consistency	Measured outwardly by liking, following and defending	Measured outwardly by induced actions
What you are	What you do	What you know
100% dictated by you	75% dictated by you	50% dictated by you
Makes you happy or sad	Makes you rich or poor	Makes you good or bad
Developed over a lifetime	Developed over a season	Developed over a lunchtime
Integrity	Credentials	Testimonials
Honesty	Accolades	Buying decisions
Compassion	Image	Referrals
Ability	Awards	Endorsements
Achievements	Qualifications	Credibility
Your hopes	Your promises	Your delivery
Your aims	Your professionalism, your standards and your work ethic	Your integrity
Your values	Your car and your house	First impressions
The garment	The label	How people read and interpret the label
Your private face	Your public face	The public perception of you
Your aptitude	Your products and services	Clients pleased or disappointed
Your preparedness	Your business card and your elevator speech	Irritated or enlightened
Your taste	Your clothes, your accessories	Your aura and your look
Your messiness or tidiness	Your office, your desk, your décor	Organised or sloppy
Your technophilia/technophobia	Your gadgets, your technology and your systems	Out of date or up to date
Your appreciation of design	Your website, your logo and your stationery	Classy or 'naff'
Your experience	The impression of dealing with you	The experience of dealing with you
What makes you think, talk and act the way you do	How other people think you think, talk and act	How you make other people think, talk and act

It is relatively easy to distinguish between reputation and character, as one is inside and one is outside. The line between your personal brand and your reputation is more complex. Branding is a hot topic – you just have to look at the thousands of strong, well-known brands across the world. Corporate branding is a major expenditure on the balance sheet. And personal branding is becoming more and more important.

Your personal brand is your public face. It's how everything on the inside comes out. It directly influences your reputation, which is what other people think of you and say about you behind your back. You can control to some extent what others think about you, providing you give them the right messages and cues.

> *"Your personal brand is a combination of all the messages you give out that makes people think the way they do about you."*
> **Lesley Everett[5]**, personal branding expert
> and founder of Walking Tall

In order to understand reputation, it is crucial to appreciate the role of your personal brand. You see, like your reputation, whether you realise it or not, you already have a personal brand. **Your personal brand is everything that connects you to the outside world and that comes from deep within you.** This book is not so much about character and personal brand. You just need to know that both make up your reputation, which is what you are known for, and it positions you as the 'go to' expert in your field. It is a measure of the control you have over how others perceive you.

"Reputation ~ the beliefs or opinions that are generally held about someone or something."
The Compact Oxford English Dictionary

"Reputation is the general opinion of the public towards you."
Wikipedia – free encyclopaedia

"Reputation ~ how much respect or admiration someone or something receives, based on past behaviour or character."
Cambridge Advanced Learner's Dictionary

Here is a mini reputation quiz. It consists of twelve questions, your answers to which will give you a much better insight into the state of your brand. They will also lay the foundations for the work you need to do to become the expert you want to be. May I suggest you take a sheet of blank paper and give them some thought for 10-20 mins? These questions are not easy to answer without a certain degree of thought and introspection.

1. *What would you say you stood for in your business and personal life?*

2. *From what you know, what do people think of you?*

3. *How would you describe your reputation and your status in your business community?*

4. *When your name is mentioned in your absence, what do you suppose people are thinking and saying?*

5. *What would you say defines you?*

6. *What are you currently known for?*

7. *What do you want to be known for if this is different to your answer above?*

8. *As far as you can tell, what exactly is <u>your</u> reputation?*

9. *How do you position yourself in your business life?*

10. *What are you currently doing or not doing that is enhancing your personal brand?*

11. *What are you currently doing or not doing that is destroying your personal brand?*

12. *Who are you associating with? What does your network say about you?*

The degree to which you can come up with accurate answers to these questions will reflect how far you actually are in control of your reputation. If you don't do introspection, may I suggest that you seek out and find those really good people around you who can help tease these answers out of you?

> *"Choose a good reputation over good riches, for being held in high esteem is better than having silver or gold."*
> **The Bible, Proverbs 22:1**

Reputation Starts from the Inside

If you're going to build your reputation, you've got to start from the inside. My definition of your REP (reputation) is the **Reason Everyone Pays** you **attention, respect** and, of course, **money**. To get to the point where they do this, you must understand how a reputation is made.

It starts by thinking about who you are. This is actually four people. On the inside is **who you really are**. This is your inner character, that even you don't know completely about. Close to this, but more on the outside like your personal brand (since it is the image you think you project to the outside world) is **who you think you are**. Who you think you are is usually a reflection of the cues and feedback you get from others around you. Starting to look outwards is your desired reputation, or **who you want to be**, as well as your current reputation, which is **who other people think you are**.

If you know the word congruency, you'll see that if all of these circles become one, you are a person who is truly 'at one' with yourself. In other words, what everyone sees is what they get. For the most authentic, most convincing and easily maintained personal reputation, you should be aiming to bring these elements as closely in line as you can.

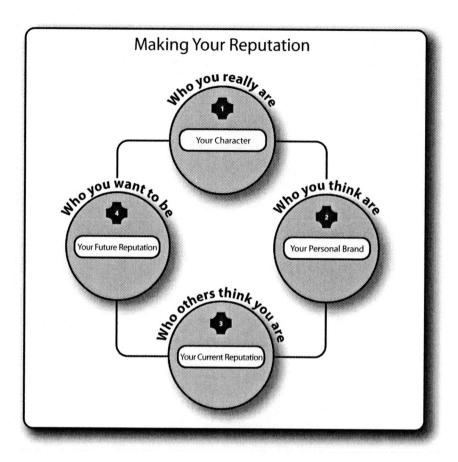

To develop an authentic, genuine reputation, you must start from the inside and work outwards. Unless you want to be known for something you are not, your reputation will always reflect your inner character.

> "The way to gain a good reputation is to endeavour to be what you desire to appear."
> **Socrates,** ancient Greek philosopher (470-399 BC)

Successful reputations tend to be authentic. What separates you from your competition is connected to the person you are inside.

Your personal attitude can make or break your business. Having the right motives is essential – people don't take long to see through a façade. You need to be genuine about changing yourself to meet your branding target, if you want your reputation to reflect that branding.

> *"You can fool some of the people all of the time, and all of the people some of the time, but you cannot fool all of the people all of the time."*
> **Abraham Lincoln**, 16th president of USA (1809 - 1865)

As a long-term strategy, it is almost impossible to pretend to be someone you are not. So before you start designing your reputation you need to become very self-aware of who you are and what you stand for.

The Johari Window

One of the best models for this is the Johari Window, developed by American psychologists Joseph Luft and Harry Ingham in the 1950s. Incidentally, the term Johari comes from their two first names, Joe and Harry!

The Window represents information within and about yourself. This comprises your motivations, skills, intentions, views, experience, attitudes and feelings and is seen from four differing perspectives.

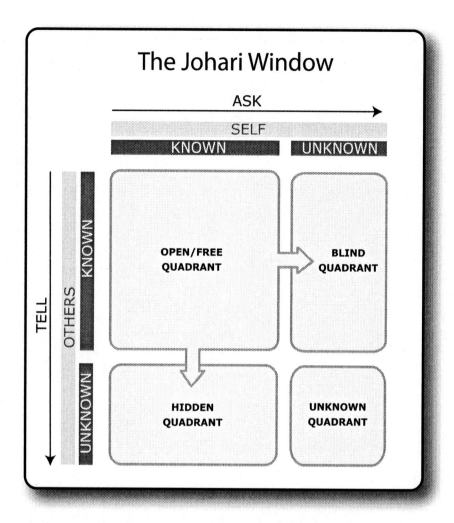

This model is worth unpacking, because it will give you deep insight into who you are, what is known about you and how people perceive you. Essentially, the four quadrants describe what is known and not known about you, both from your perspective and an outside perspective.

The Known Quadrant

This sector, often called the open or free area, represents what you know about yourself and what other people know about you. When you are making your mark in a new role, breaking into new territory, starting a new job, working with a fresh team or embarking on a new project, this area can be small. That is because the people you are working with, and for, often know very little about you. As far as your reputation goes, this is not good news.

Remember your reputation is what people think about you and how they perceive you. If they have very little to go on, the information is scant and their perceptions are limited. People make up their minds about you based on what they know about you. If you want to influence what they think and do and say, you must give them the right messages, the right cues and the right data. To put it simply, if you want them to like you and trust you, they have to know you.

Think about this – if people don't know too much about you, they'll either make up their minds on incomplete information, seek out information from (perhaps) unreliable and uncontrolled sources, or make up information themselves. All of this means a lot of hearsay, gossip, rumour and fantasy. The strongest reputations are those where the individual has carefully controlled what people see, and as a result, controlled what they think and do and say.

All studies show that the more this open/free area is developed, the greater the communication, compliance, co-operation and productivity. You can expand this in two ways - horizontally into the blind area and vertically into the hidden area. You can move more into the blind area by asking others about what they think/

hear/believe about you. (This not only gives you the chance to correct them if they're wrong, but helps you find out more about yourself so you can correct yourself!). And you can move into the hidden area by telling others more about yourself.

The Blind Quadrant

This is also known as your ignorance! If you are thick-skinned and have issues or undesirable traits that others see in you but you cannot see or admit to yourself, then you are operating in the dark. The darkness represents things you are in denial about or things that other people are withholding from you. 'Thick-skinned' people tend to have a large blind area.

You will never develop a strong reputation for the things you want to be known for if you are not aware of your shortcomings and you are blissfully ignorant of what other people really know and think about you. If you can solicit feedback by asking others what they know of you, what they think about you and how you come across, then you increase what you know about yourself (your self-awareness). Only this way can you begin to eradicate your faults, smooth off your rough edges and create the reputation you truly desire.

The Hidden Quadrant

This represents things you know about yourself but do not reveal to others. Everyone has secrets, fears, sensitivities, unseen agendas and even hidden, devious intentions. Some of these are very natural, and you have your reasons for not sharing them. Some things should rightly be kept hidden - usually the inner feelings, fears and information that have no bearing on your professional life. But there is a case to be made for releasing certain information in the interests of co-operation and mutual understanding.

If you can share more of yourself, disclose information and tell others things about you, then you can increase what others know of you. If you can do this in a controlled and organised way, you are essentially taking charge of your reputation.

> *"I am a poor mendicant. All my earthly possessions consist of six spinning wheels, a can of goat's milk, six homespun loincloths, one towel – and my reputation, which cannot be worn."*
> **Mahatma Gandhi,** in reply to a Customs officer who asked whether he had anything to declare.

The Unknown Quadrant

You may have latent abilities. You may have talents inside you that you don't even know you possess. You may have an aptitude that, because of a lack of opportunity, training, confidence or encouragement, has not been realised. You may have subconscious fears, repressed feelings or even an unknown illness that you are blissfully unaware of. You may be carrying emotional baggage in the form of conditioned behaviour or attitudes from your childhood. All of these represent your unknown area.

If you want to cultivate a strong reputation, your job is to diminish and shrink your unknown area. This will help you minimise any possibility of sabotaging your own reputation. Many potentially great people have been undone by a failure to acknowledge and explore any deeper aspects of their personality and behaviour. This is especially common in younger people and those who lack experience or self-belief.

All the great books on leadership will say that leadership is simply influencing. If you want to influence your people and your clients and your contacts, then you want to develop a reputation for trust, credibility, strong communication, openness and a desire to help. You can do this by ensuring people think the right things about you and also giving them the right things to think.

Remember, successful reputations tend to be authentic. What separates you from your competition is connected to the person you are inside. Having the right motives is essential – people don't take long to see through pretence. You need to be genuine about changing yourself if you want your reputation to reflect that self.

> *"If I take care of my character,*
> *my reputation will take care of itself."*
> **Dwight L Moody**, famous US preacher (1837-1899)

Now you have a thorough understanding of reputations, you are ready to begin designing your own.

Section 2: DESIGNING REPUTATIONS

Laying the Foundation
....

The important starting point in developing a particular reputation is to acknowledge you've got one already. In fact, you've got several! And if you doubt you have even a single reputation, consider this. Human beings are naturally judgemental. They have opinions, thoughts and feelings. When people talk about you behind your back, your reputation will come out. Face it - you've had a reputation since the day you were born: "What a beautiful baby!"

If you think you need a good reputation, you're right. If you think you don't already have a reputation, you're wrong. From a business perspective, your clients, customers, employers, prospects and associates are judging you every time your name is mentioned. It's now well known from all the research on buying and selling that people make decisions emotionally, then justify them afterwards with logic. When they have a problem or need, they will generally choose you *as a person* to solve or fulfil it, not you *as a robot* that does a job mechanically.

The instincts people use to make judgments about you can be subtly influenced on many levels and in many ways. If people make up their minds from the cues they receive from their surroundings, then it is up to you to make sure they receive the correct cues.

So let us first investigate what these cues might be by thinking about the kind of reputation you've got right now. The reputation you want to build for yourself depends to some extent on who you currently are and how you're currently perceived. But the good news is that you can change that!

Put another way, the reputation you want to develop needs a foundation. The direction you take to get there very much depends on where you're starting from.

As you take stock to ascertain your current position, you have to take a hard look at the inside. In this respect, your reputation (what others think of you) follows very similar rules to your self-esteem (what you think of yourself). And the difference between how you see yourself and how others see you is what I call **The Reputation Gap.**

The Reputation Gap helps you answer two huge questions:

1.   WHAT IS YOUR REPUTATION?
2.   IS IT THE ONE YOU WANT?

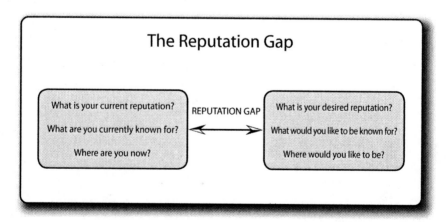

If there is any distance between what you are currently known for and what you'd like to be known for, then you have a **Reputation Gap** which you must bridge. If there is any space between your current success, wealth, influence or reputation and where you would like it to be, then you have a **Reputation Gap** which you can close.

To decide your current position, and establish the foundation on which your reputation will be built or changed, it's very useful to start with a personal inventory. In other words, what have you got? What tools are in your toolbox? What do people think of you right now?

You have some great unique qualities, but you must dig down deep and find out what they are. Remember this is not your corporate or company reputation. **This is personal**, so you have to look at your own background and your own life story.

As this develops, if you find your reputation is not the one you want, this book will show you how to change that. If you really want to become the obvious expert in your field, you can do it. You simply need to follow the road map that experts before you have followed. It starts from the ground up. You don't build a big house or tower without laying really strong and deep foundations. Here's a selection of exercises to lay the foundations and determine what your reputation is right now.

> *"Character is like the foundation of a house*
> *– it is below the surface."*
> **Anon**

71

The Reality Gap Exercise

Looking back at the Johari Window, and the four people inside you (who you really are, who you think you are, who you want to be and who others think you are), you can get a clear picture of what you're currently working with.

This exercise looks at the gap between how you think others see you (your perceived reputation) and how you see yourself (your self-esteem). Remember this is one piece of the puzzle – you will be verifying your answers with other exercises.

In the table opposite there are 28 areas of your business and personal life about which you have an opinion of your performance. Simply go down the list and rank yourself on each side with a score from 1 to 10 based on how you rate yourself and how you think others rate you.

For the full range of reputation building exercises, including worksheets, question banks, evaluation tools, supplementary information and recommended reading, there is an accompanying 'Reputation Building Manual'. Go to www.thetripsystem.com for more details.

Obviously this table helps identify areas where there is a disparity between what others think of you and what you think of yourself. To interpret the results, note the following points:

(turn to page 74)

The Reality Gap

Your Reputation .... Your Self-esteem
What Others Think of You ..... What You Think of Yourself
How Others See You .... How You See Yourself
External .... Internal

LOW   HIGH

		1	2	3	4	5	6	7	8	9	10	

	The way you talk	
	The way you walk	
	The way you sing	
	The way you look naked	
	The way you dance	
	The way you network	
	The way you treat your clients and customers	
	The way you dress	
	How fit you are	
	How healthy you are	
	How organised you are	
	How punctual you are	
	How much fun you are	
	How clever you are	
	How reliable you are	
	How positive and optimistic you are	
	How negative and pessimistic you are	
	How forgiving you are	
	How patient you are	
	How good you are at your job	
	How good you are at your hobby/sport	
	How well you write	
	How well you create ideas	
	How well you relate to authority	
	How well you relate to your colleagues	
	How well you relate to subordinates	
	How you handle challenge and adversity	
	How persistent you are	

	ADD UP YOUR TOTALS HERE	

1. The wider the gap between the two scores, the greater the gap between how you see yourself and how others see you.

2. A significantly higher total on your self-esteem (the right side) may indicate two things. One, you think that others see you as 'less' than you really are. You think they don't see the 'true you' and as a result you feel you don't have the reputation you deserve. Two, you are over-confident in your abilities and qualities, and 'over-egg' your reputation.

3. A significantly lower total on your self-esteem obviously indicates you are better than you think you are, so you need to change how you perceive yourself.

The Elimination Exercise

When I was deciding my own focus and what I wanted to be known for, there was one exercise that really got me on the right track, and it was one I devised for myself. It didn't give me the whole picture but combined with other career management exercises and goal setting strategies, it helped me lay the foundations for my success. It should do the same for you.

This one is especially good if there are a lot of zones you operate in, be they sectors, geographical regions, knowledge areas or channels of delivery (consulting, coaching, servicing, training, managing, leading, speaking, etc). The power of this exercise is that it helps you eliminate things that you might be good at or love doing, but ultimately will not make you successful.

> *"Your success and happiness lie within you. External conditions are the accidents of life, its outer trappings."*
> **Helen Keller**, American author and educator who was blind and deaf (1880 - 1968)

Draw up a three column table like the one below. One column is for things you love doing, another is for things you're really good at and the third is where the demand (and therefore the money) is. Anything that appears on all three lists gives you a strong indication of your purpose in life – what you're meant to be doing.

PASSION What I Love Doing	SKILLS What I'm Really Good At	DEMAND What Pays Me Money

Again, for this exercise and more, see the accompanying 'Reputation Building Manual'. Go to www.thetripsystem.com for more details.

Complete it with all the traits, skills, passions, interests and desires you can think of. Then simply look at what is on all three lists. You see, if you're operating outside what you're good at, outside what you love doing or outside where the demand is, you will struggle to create the reputation you really want. Why? Because you've got to be good at something to make your name. Or you've got to really love something to make your name in it. Or you've got to give people what they really want to make your name. Of course, there is one other way to be successful: to be really lucky! Do you want to leave it to chance?

Roger Hamilton[6], Asia's leading wealth consultant and founder of Wealth Dynamics calls this working 'in your flame' – doing the thing you were born to do. Penny Power[7], co-founder of Ecademy, the world's largest online networking organisation, simply calls it being in the flow. It's where you bring the most energy, purpose and leverage to bear for optimum results.

When I did this, I found that it was in two skill areas (presenting and writing) and one content area (relationship marketing) that my destiny laid. Not coaching, not sales, not HR, not team development, not leadership and not traditional training. The fact that I could do these other things, or knew something about them or could speak about them was actually hindering my development. The power is in the elimination as well as the identification.

It may help you to know some of the other things this exercise helped me eliminate. These are things I loved doing: playing the guitar and piano, juggling, travelling the world and internet marketing. These are the things I could do well: training, coaching (particularly in the sporting domain - I'm actually qualified to coach seven sports), and after dinner speaking.

It will also be interesting for you to see what areas, skills or activities *that you're currently doing* appear on only one list or not at all. One of mine was working for somebody else. That's the position I was in, but only appeared on one column – Demand! And that demand came from the organisation I was working for. Another was selling. Selling was definitely in the demand column, but I was not particularly good at it, and really didn't like it. It's a necessary skill which I've worked on, but it hasn't been a core element of my career since I realised this. Yet I seemed to find myself in selling roles, wondering why I wasn't having fun!

Here are a few more ways you can nail down who, where and what you are right now by identifying your greatest skills and abilities.

The 'Ideal' Exercise

Write down what type of work really excites you. You're looking for your ideal job, role, project or client. List your roles and link them to your attributes. You are not just, for example, a banker or an accountant. You are a certain type of professional, and these questions will help. These and other key questions are available in the accompanying 'Reputation Building Manual'. Go to www. thetripsystem.com for more details.

- What are you known for?
- What experience do you have?
- What are you most proud of in your working or personal life?
- What have you achieved that is worth boasting about?
- What are you passionate about in your work?
- What kind of work and/or clients gives you the most satisfaction?
- What was the most interesting project you've worked on recently?

The SWOT Analysis

You might be very familiar with this, but you may not have used it before in laying the foundations for your personal reputation. SWOT stands for Strengths, Weaknesses, Opportunities and Threats. This builds on the positives and looks at ways of converting your weaknesses and threats into strengths and opportunities.

Used in a business context, it can show you how to develop sustainable niches in your market. Used in a personal context, it helps you develop your career in a way that takes best advantage of your talents, abilities and opportunities. Do a separate analysis for your career and your life goals. (For the full range of reputation building exercises, including worksheets, question banks, evaluation tools, supplementary information and recommended reading, there is an accompanying 'Reputation Building Manual. Go to www.thetripsystem.com for more details.)

SWOT ANALYSIS TABLE

STRENGTHS	WEAKNESSES
What do others see as your strengths?	Where do you have fewer resources than others?
What unique resources can you draw on?	What flaws might trip you up in the future?
What do you do better than most other people?	What could you possibly improve?
What advantages do you have over your competitors?	What are other people likely to see as your weaknesses?
OPPORTUNITIES	THREATS
What good opportunities are open to you?	What threats could be harming you?
What trends could you take advantage of?	What is your competition doing particularly well?

You should consider this from an internal perspective and also from the point of view of your clients and people in your market. In looking at your strengths, think about them in relation to your rivals. For example, if all your competitors provide online services, then this is not a strength in the market, it is a necessity. With opportunities and threats, be mindful of any changes in technology, markets, government legislation and lifestyle trends.

The Core Values Exercise

This exercise will help you if you plan to develop your reputation through character traits, which you will learn more about later. You simply have to identify your core values. A core value is something you really believe in, something that is truly important to you. Many say that core values are discovered rather than invented. They are usually based on moral or ethical principles with little room for deviation or change, whatever the circumstances.

Identifying your core values opens the door to understanding, on a deeper level, what truly matters to you and motivates you. Knowing and applying them in your daily life is a powerful route to being more effective in the face of difficult or challenging situations.

Here are some examples of corporate values associated with companies you may recognise:

The Body Shop	*No testing of cosmetics on animals*
Sony	*Being a pioneer, not following others*
BMW	*Not sacrificing quality to price*

Walt Disney   *The worth of the family*

Procter & Gamble *Respect for the individual; doing what's right for the long-term*

The Twelve Core Values defined in Cub Scouting to guide the development of character in boys		
Compassion	Co-operation	Faith
Health and Fitness	Citizenship	Perseverence
Positive Attitude	Respect	Resourcefulness
Honesty	Responsibility	Courage

Depending on where you look, there are around 70 core personal values from which you should be able to identify between five and seven that hold true for you. Any more than that tends to become difficult to monitor and sustain. A list of the main ones is given below. You'll note that some seem to evoke the same interpretation, e.g. truth and honesty, or joy and happiness. However, specific words may suit you, your character and your aspirations.

Core Personal Values Table

Joy	Recognition	Happiness	Power
Influence	Wealth	Justice	Fame
Family	Balance	Status	Control
Integrity	Wisdom	Success	Learning
Truth	Creativity	Authenticity	Strength
Play	Dignity	Courage	Peace
Innovation	Honour	Accountability	Love
Integrity	Flexibility	Relationship	Loyalty
Security	Learning	Commitment	Persistence
Fun	Faith	Fairness	Spirituality
Honesty	Cooperation	Order	Collaboration
Respect	Humour	Dependability	Contribution
Adventure	Compassion	Quality	Justice
Support	Trust	Freedom	Resourcefulness
Friendship	Service	Connectedness	Charity
Understanding	Dedication	Caring	Purposefulness
Generosity	Kindness	Beauty	Excellence

© Rob Brown 2007   www.thetripsystem.com

From this table, pick out five or six that really ring true for you. You do this by asking yourself what is the most important thing in your life? Then, what's the next most important thing? This will help you decide what you are passionate about in work and life, and what you will hold to when the seas get a little rough.

Remember your character is reflected through your actions, thoughts and words to the outside world, and this is what makes or breaks your reputation. There is no substitute for character. You can buy almost everything in today's world, except character.

Note that core values are not like company slogans or mottos such as 'The no.1 company for customer care'. These are usually thought up by marketing people and often bear little relation to how the company actually works. They are imposed, whereas core values emanate from the depths of an organisation's soul!

> *"A man's reputation is the opinion people have of him;*
> *his character is what he really is."*
> **Jack Miner,** Canadian naturalist, author and lecturer
> (1865-1944)

The Guy in the Glass

When you get what you want in your struggle for pelf*,
And the world makes you King for a day,
Then go to the mirror and look at yourself,
And see what that guy has to say.

82

For it isn't your Father or Mother or Wife,
Who judgement upon you must pass.
The feller whose verdict counts most in your life
Is the guy staring back from the glass.
He's the feller to please, never mind all the rest,
For he's with you clear up to the end,
And you've passed your most dangerous, difficult test
If the guy in the glass is your friend.
You may be like Jack Horner and 'chisel' a plum,
And think you're a wonderful guy,
But the man in the glass says you're only a bum
If you can't look him straight in the eye.
You can fool the whole world down the pathway of years,
And get pats on the back as you pass,
But your final reward will be heartaches and tears
If you've cheated the guy in the glass.
by Dale Wimbrow, 1934

*The word 'pelf' is not a misprint. It means money or wealth, usually ill-gotten, derived from Old French pelfe and pelfre, meaning reward gained from plunder or contest or achievements.

For a more detailed treatment of this Core Values Exercise and other reputation building exercises, including worksheets, question banks, evaluation tools, supplementary information and recommended reading, there is an accompanying 'Reputation Building Manual'. Go to www.thetripsystem.com for more details.

The Employment Exercise

Look at what has been written about you. Get out your recent CVs, job applications and performance evaluations.

- What are they saying about you?
- What are you saying about yourself?
- What phrases are they using?
- What phrases are you using?
- Do you notice any patterns?
- Are there descriptions that keep popping up?
- What action words are being used?

Action words are what employers look out for and latch onto. Opposite is a list of 184 action-oriented words commonly found on the best CVs and Résumés throughout the world. Which of them are on yours? These say what you can do (because you've done it before!).

These are all strong verbs that help define you and what you're about. They will also help you create the language and vocabulary you want to be known for. Speaking with this kind of language with those people you want to influence will surely have a positive effect on your reputation!

Again, this list and a full range of reputation building exercises, including worksheets, question banks, evaluation tools, supplementary information and recommended reading, is in the accompanying 'Reputation Building Manual'. Go to www. thetripsystem.com for more details.

The Best Action-Oriented Words To Craft Your Reputation

Accelerated	Critiqued	Innovated	Rehabilitated
Achieved	Cut	Inspected	Remodelled
Acted	Delegated	Installed	Reorganised
Adapted	Delivered	Instituted	Repaired
Addressed	Demonstrated	Instructed	Represented
Administered	Demystified	Integrated	Researched
Advised	Designed	Interpreted	Resolved (problems)
Allocated	Developed	Interviewed	Restored
Analysed	Diagnosed	Introduced	Retrieved
Appraised	Directed	Invented	Reviewed
Approved	Dispatched	Investigated	Revitalised
Arbitrated	Drafted	Launched	Scheduled
Arranged	Edited	Lectured	Screened
Assembled	Educated	Maintained	Set goals
Assessed	Eliminated	Managed	Set up
Assigned	Enabled	Marketed	Shaped
Assisted	Encouraged	Mediated	Simplified
Attained	Engineered	Moderated	Sold
Audited	Enlisted	Monitored	Solved
Authored	Established	Motivated	Spearheaded
Balanced	Evaluated	Negotiated	Specified
Budgeted	Examined	Operated	Spoke
Built	Executed	Organised	Stimulated
Calculated	Exhibited	Originated	Streamlined
Catalogued	Expanded	Overhauled	Strengthened
Chaired	Expedited	Oversaw	Succeeded
Clarified	Explained	Performed	Summarised
Classified	Extracted	Persuaded	Supervised
Coached	Fabricated	Pioneered	Supported
Collaborated	Facilitated	Planned	Surveyed
Collected	Familiarised	Prepared	Systemised
Communicated	Fashioned	Prioritised	Tabulated
Compiled	Forecasted	Processed	Trained
Computed	Formulated	Produced	Transformed
Conceived	Founded	Programmed	Translated
Conceptualised	Generated	Projected	Trimmed
Conducted	Guided	Promoted	Tripled
Consolidated	Headed	Provided	Uncovered
Contracted	Identified	Publicised	Unified
Converted	Illustrated	Purchased	Unravelled
Convinced	Implemented	Recommended	Upgraded
Coordinated	Improved	Reconciled	Validated
Corresponded	Increased	Recorded	Widened
Counselled	Influenced	Recruited	Won
Created	Informed	Referred	Wrote

The Observation Exercise

Observe how people act and react around you. Notice how other people, particularly colleagues and business associates, describe you when they introduce you to others. They often use powerful language which is positive - maybe more positive than you have been using yourself. Are people respectful, polite or dismissive? Do they seek you or do you seek them?

Compare this to how people react and talk about the kind of people you admire. What's the difference? This is an awareness exercise – these interactions are taking place under your nose every day - you just haven't noticed. Be more aware of what compliance, resistance or interest you induce in different situations. Do external contacts tend to treat and talk to you differently compared to internal colleagues? Are you someone different in social situations than work situations?

The Courageous Questions Exercise

If you want to know what other people think of you, there's a simple way to find out. ASK! This will help you identify what makes you 'you', what makes you good and what might be holding you back. The trick is in asking courageously and in asking the right people.

If you're going to solicit the opinions of people who you care about (and presumably who care about you) then you've got to be open to straight talk. You must be open to whatever your friends, peers, clients, customers, associates, superiors, mentors and employees say and think are your greatest strengths.

It helps to let people know why you're asking – some people wouldn't know how to handle your questions coming out of nowhere. Here are a few scripts and phrases that might help you set the scene:

- *I've been thinking about a new career direction recently, and would appreciate a little feedback on a couple of things...*

- *I'm doing some personal development work and need to ask a few close friends and associates about how I come across...*

- *Could I pick your brains on a couple of personal development challenges I'm going through at the moment?*

- *Could you help me with something? I've got some questions I need to ask someone who knows me quite well...*

- *Could I ask your advice on a couple of things I've been working through recently?*

- *I wonder if you could help me with something? I'm working through a professional development programme and need to solicit a few opinions from people who know me fairly well...*

- *I need someone who could give me some really honest feedback on a couple of things...*

The Survey Exercise

This is a more structured approach where you solicit feedback from whoever is affected by what you do. The best way is to design a mini-questionnaire or survey and get them to fill it in. Like the previous exercise, you'll need to set the scene and give them suitable reasons to secure their involvement and frank feedback.

So instead of asking them outright, you prepare a little two pager for them to take away and complete in their own time. You are looking for people who know you enough to give useful feedback, who are honest enough to tell it how it is and are organised and conscientious enough to complete the task. These might also be people who have a vested interest in your success, such as line managers, partners, friends, key clients and contacts.

The Aptitude Test

An aptitude or psychometric test is a fabulous way to assess your strengths, weaknesses and skills. There are hundreds of these available. Many can be found on the internet and some are free! Do several and see what comes up repeatedly. The results will give you some clear descriptions of what type of person you are.

Other Approaches

Here are a few more avenues of exploration if you struggle with any of the tasks above, or need to flesh your findings out further. It's always good to seek corroborative evidence if you lack confidence in your findings or if you want to be absolutely sure that you have done a comprehensive job in unearthing your unique skills and attributes. Here are three ways to do just that:

1. There are lots of great self-development audio programmes out there. *Listen to them.*
2. There are lots of great articles and books on discovering your strengths. *Read them.*
3. There are lots of great coaches and mentors out there. *Work with them.*

So where does all this introspection and self-analysis leave you? You should now have a really strong idea of who you are, what you stand for and where your passions and strengths lie. You should have direction. You should know what you want to work on and how you want to be known. It's time to decide – what reputation do you want? The major consideration here is your **Unique Value Proposition**, which comes through *specialising* or *niching*.

The Power of Niche Positioning to Develop Your Reputation

So, you want to put together the reputation you desire and deserve. Until now, you've probably left your reputation to chance. You've let other people think things about you without either knowing or believing you could influence them. But now you can see that it doesn't have to be this way.

You have a certain element of control about how other people see you and perceive you. If they make up their minds about you based on certain things, then you know that if you change and influence those things, you can alter your reputation for the good.

Looking at the business aspects of your reputation, it is very unlikely that the product or service you offer is unique. But now you realise that if you can create a special and desirable reputation, you can set yourself and what you are marketing apart from the rest. This is why you must position yourself carefully.

Positioning is crucial if you want to develop a strong reputation. Positioning is deciding what space you want to occupy, both in terms of your marketplace and the minds of your target audience, and taking up that position. Positioning helps you to stand out from the crowd.

You must clearly communicate your position to your target audience:

> *"Great communicators have an appreciation for positioning. They understand the people they're trying to reach and what they can and can't hear. They send their message in through an open door rather than trying to push it through a wall."*
> **John Kotter**, former professor at Harvard Business School

If you've paid any attention to **The 21st Century Laws of Business**, you'll know that you must have a profile in one form or another. Given that you can't be all things to all people, your best chance for success lies in defining niches or specialisations. This allows you to differentiate yourself and stand out in an aggressive and cluttered marketplace. It ensures people come to you instead of you having to find them.

> ## Specialisation = Profile = Differentiation = Niche = Profits

Any kind of specialisation can be frightening. It's almost like getting married. The incredible thing about marriage is not so much that you say 'yes' to somebody, it's that you say 'no' to everybody else. From a business perspective, you worry that narrowing your focus gives you a lack of options, but what it actually does is bring more and different options.

There are six great benefits of positioning yourself:

1. It Makes Selling Yourself Easier

If you *like* cold calling, then ignore this one. If you like spending money on advertising and telemarketing campaigns, ignore this one. Quite simply, a strong reputation reverses the energy in your marketing from push to pull. You draw clients in instead of having to go after them. You pull them towards you instead of pushing them to buy.

 Shay McConnon[8] and his wife Margaret run People First International, a people development and training consultancy. Between them they have produced over 20 books, which gives them a very powerful and unique reputation in the market place. Shay admits to having done little or no marketing for the last few years, and still turns over a very healthy profit with work booked into the diary more than 18 months in advance.

2. People Perceive Value

When people clearly see what you do and the value of your products and services to them, you immediately distinguish yourself from the rest of the herd who want to compete on price. Your perceived value means you will most likely be paid more and be in demand. In addition, people will be less likely to negotiate and haggle with your fees and prices. Why? They want to do business with you *despite* rather than *because of* cost. Remember that price is only ever an objection in the absence of value.

> *"Price is what you pay, value is what you get."*
> **Warren Buffett**, American investor
> and CEO of Berkshire Hathaway

When people can see the value you bring, they are altogether less likely to question the cost. You can make this value apparent through testimonials, third-party endorsements and great reputation marketing.

 Imagine your kitchen is flooding. You need a plumber. You reach for the Yellow Pages. You pick up the phone and dial a number. When a plumber answers the phone, you are likely to ask him two questions: "How much will it cost?" and "How soon can you get here?" Contrast this with a different approach to the same problem. This time you call a friend and ask if they know any good plumbers. They recommend someone who's recently worked with them and did a great job. They give you his number. You pick up the phone and dial it. You are likely

to ask just one question: "How soon can you get here?"
Do you see how people are less likely to haggle on price
when recommended to come to you?

3. It Sets You Up as the 'Go To' Professional

You are front of mind, which means that when they want a product or service that you provide, they think of you first. This overcomes the 'feast and famine' problem that many professionals face, because there is always a stream of highly qualified prospects wanting to do business with you.

Andy Mouncey[9] is famous as the Arch to Arc Endurance Triathlete. That means he ran 80 miles from Marble Arch in London, swam the English Channel and biked 270 miles to the Arc de Triomphe in Paris. He made the fastest time ever. It helps his coaching and speaking business because more people know him and know about him than he knows about them. When people want a motivational speaker or coach to improve their performance, Andy is spoken and written about so much that they come to him first.

4. It Educates Your Marketplace

A strong specialisation means you can filter out unqualified leads and irrelevant inquiries because people are very clear about exactly what you do and who you do it for. More importantly, people are clear on what you won't do. In addition, your message will be easy to understand and more memorable, and any marketing you do will be more focused and targeted.

Steve is a partner in the personal injury department of a mid-sized regional law firm. He wanted to steer the department away from low level, low margin insurance claims to more complex and unusual cases which fully utilised his department's expertise. He planned a series of alliances built up with legal professionals in other firms, and a campaign of article writing and public speaking. As a result, Steve was able to minimise requests and tenders for the wrong kind of work, pass on referrals to other firms and also attract more of the kind of work he was excellent at and wanted to do. The more he did, the better he did it and the more well known he became.

5. It Makes You More Exclusive

There is always the top 10% of the market place who are willing to pay premium prices for the best possible advisers, providers and suppliers in a certain field. As my friend Peter Thomson says, you just have to hold your breath! Your presumed expertise makes you more likely to be chosen. This allows you to attract the very best clients and customers, and charge premium fees for your work.

The top 10% of the people in your field will earn 90% of the available money. Are they nine times better? No. One of my competitors in the world of relationship marketing commands a speaking fee of £25,000 per day. This is ever so slightly beyond my fee, and when I see him speak I do not wonder why people pay him so much, because he is good. But certainly not five times better than I am. His reputation pays him those fees, and when mine is similarly

strong, there is no reason why I will not be able to charge the same fees.

6. It Increases Your Productivity

Most professionals are not comfortable with marketing, and they dislike paperwork and administration. When you establish yourself as the obvious expert in your field, people will come to you. This reduces your marketing efforts and costs and you can outsource the lower level tasks with the extra revenue you generate. You can also let go of lots of other things and focus on your strengths.

 Sandra is a life coach. Three years ago, her five day working week looked like this: two days marketing (networking, follow-up calls, cold calls, proposals and writing), two days delivering (coaching), half a day administrating (accounts, e-mails, etc.) and half a day learning (researching, self-development). Now she works a four-and-a-half day week: three days delivering, half a day marketing, half a day administrating and half a day learning. Because she is now working more on fee-generating activities (coaching) she can actually outsource some marketing and administration work, which frees her up to earn even more money and do the things she loves to do, i.e. working with clients.

95

How to Niche

There are four main ways you can position yourself as a specialist and set yourself apart from the crowd. You can niche by:

1. **What You Do - Your Offering**
2. **How You Do It – Your Client Experience**
3. **Where You Do It – Your Geographical Sphere**
4. **Whom You Do It For – Your Target Audience**

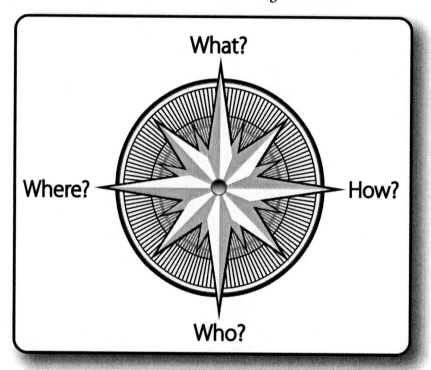

Very few people 'make it' as a generalist these days. People tend to look for and pay for some kind of expertise. To position yourself properly and craft the right reputation to make this happen, you need to 'go deep'. You need to niche. You need to specialise. Let's look at these four niches in more detail.

1. What You Do - Your Offering

If your business card says more than one offering or more than one title, you would be well advised to 'pick a lane'! People can get confused. Their focus can be dissipated by having too many things to think about. They generally want the best they can find and look out for the ultimate 'go to' professional to solve their problems. Too many 'solopreneurs' are coaches, authors, trainers, speakers, mentors and all-round fantastic people. Too many management consultants offer change management, team development, sales and marketing expertise, interim management and an opinion on pretty much everything your business needs. Too many speakers are experts on motivation, leadership, presentation skills, negotiation skills, sales skills and people development. Too many financial planners and advisors claim to specialise in mortgages, healthcare, pensions, savings and investments.

Can you see what is happening here? These people are basically saying to you, *"The answer is yes I can. Now what's the question?"* Before you get too complacent if you're in an 'employed' role, be warned that too many accountants, lawyers and bankers fall into a similar trap. I'm only just beginning to see specialist public sector tax advisers, specialist employment tribunal lawyers and specialist commercial property bankers.

Given the wealth of knowledge around our planet today, it is virtually impossible to specialise in multiple areas, the way people did 10 and 20 years ago. Leonardo da Vinci has been described as the man who wanted to know everything. This 'Renaissance man' was an artist, scientist and engineer. He was an all-round genius whose paintings and inventions changed the world. Have you ever stopped to think why there are no more polymaths (people of great learning in several fields of study) in the world today?

Consider this dilemma. You need a specific heart operation. Would you go to a general heart surgeon who knows a lot about the heart? Or would you go to a particular heart surgeon who has performed that particular operation 113 times in that particular year?

Here's another. You need some specialist cosmetic work done on your teeth. Would you go to a general dentist? Or would you feel more comfortable in the hands of a dentist who did nothing but that specialist cosmetic work, day in and day out?

Here's one more for the road. You are looking to source some funds for a business expansion. Would you go to your regular banker? Or might you be more interested to speak to a particular banker who had all the contacts, all the experience and all the expertise to handle your situation because that is all he does?

Don't get me wrong! There will always be a place for generalists. There will always be a place for broad experience. But the way the world is going, the 'go to' professionals with a strong reputation will be the ones who carve out a particular niche with a particular offering.

2. How You Do It – Your Client Experience

People say 'a bank is as good as a bank is as good as a bank'. You could substitute bank for accountant, lawyer, hotel, speaker, consultant, coach, or pretty much anything. In this surplus society, there is too much of everything. A certain blandness forms the landscape and virtually all products and services. A degree of complacency infects many business professionals. While products and services do tend to get better over time, everything seems to be moving at the same rate. **But** the client experience for all of these seems to move backwards much of the time.

You may have heard the phrase, 'Yesterday's good is tomorrow's average'. What delighted people last week, now seems ordinary this week. Customer or client satisfaction is said to be important, but be honest. Would you rather have satisfied clients or delighted clients?

There are literally hundreds of ways you can differentiate how you deliver your product or service. From your use of technology and innovation to your sense of humour and the way you treat people, think what you can do just a little bit differently to create a niche that says: 'Lots of people do this, but there's only me who does it in this unique way!'

3. Where You Do It – Your Geographical Sphere

It seems that we work longer hours and spend more time on the road than ever before. As far as I am concerned, every hour you spend on trains, planes and automobiles is time away from your existing clients and customers, your potential clients and customers, your loved ones, friends and family, your hobbies and your 'me time'.

Depending on where you live, there is probably more business within a 50 mile radius of your house than you would know what to do with. There are people in your street that probably don't know what you do, but could use your advice and expertise. Serving a particular geographical niche has many benefits, from greater productivity and focus to less wasted time travelling. There may also be particular cultural aspects that you are really good at, or can be if you know people from a certain area very well.

Think about whether you could service a certain post code or zip code? A certain town, borough or suburb? A certain county or city? A certain community? Like a laser beam, you will begin to penetrate that particular geographical market with depth and impact. This will lead to more referrals, recommendations and introductions from other people in similar locations. If you get this right, you might never need to work more than a square mile from your house!

4. Whom You Do It For – Your Target Audience

The key benefit of serving a target audience is that you can go very deep and get under their skin. So you now need to research who your target audience will be.

This tells you who you want to influence and impress. This is about who you want to work with or for. This is about attracting people to you, rather than running after any clients, customers, contacts or employers who will have you.

For instance, if you have a choice, would you put your search for the right mortgage for your next property in the hands of a general mortgage specialist, or somebody that dealt solely with first-time buyers, or young families, or senior citizens or female professionals or whatever demographic you fit?

You see, it's not that the general mortgage specialist would fail to offer you the right mortgage. It's that they wouldn't be able to understand your issues, concerns and limitations even before you had uttered them. They wouldn't quite speak your language. They might not be so sympathetic to your unique situation. One who specialised in dealing with people like you would know these things. Why? Because you are the kind of people they help, day in and day out. That's the power of having a target audience. And there is more than enough business in a narrow niche than you could ever cater for.

The more focused you are, the more efficient you can be about marketing your personal brand and creating the reputation you want with the people that count. Remember the power of specialising. You are not aiming at the whole world.

People often make the mistake of thinking they shouldn't leave anyone out of their target audience. They fear offending and putting off potential clients and customers. Their marketing then becomes vague, and in reality, attracts no one because it says nothing special and doesn't connect on an emotional level with the audience: **anyone, everybody and anybody means... nobody!**

To combat this scattered focus, ask yourself the following seven courageous questions:

1. **Who are the people you want to reach?**
2. **Who do you want to be seen with?**
3. **Whose network do you want to step into?**
4. **What social circles do you want to be a part of?**
5. **Who do you want to influence and be influenced by?**
6. **Who do you want on your radar?**
7. **Who do you want to know and be known by?**

Your answers to these questions could throw up either individuals or groups. They could throw up companies, organisations or associations. Depending on the reputation you want to create and your reason for wanting it, your target audience could be any of the following:

- **Ideal prospects – your target clients or customers** (for more business)
- **Existing clients or customers** (for more loyalty and up-selling/cross-selling opportunities)
- **Mentors and key advisers** (for help, advice and key introductions)
- **Internal connections** (for promotions, security, preferential treatment)
- **Contacts and your professional network** (for knowledge, influence and introductions)
- **Potential referral sources** (for leads, recommendations and business)
- **Social contacts** (for friends, social invitations and influence)

Focus in on who you really want to attract. Identify specific people or groups of people. Look at them and define what brings them together. What do they have in common? What are their greatest needs? How and where can you reach them?

If you can identify a target market for your message, you will accrue four worthy benefits:

1. Target Audience = Target Marketing

By targeting specific groups of people, you are narrowing the field down so that you can match what you have to what they want. They will be seeking you out instead of the other way around. By having a niche market, you will be able to keep your brand consistently visible and influence the right people in the right way. The strategy for survival is keeping yourself in the forefront of the minds of the people you want to influence and impress most. Nothing you do will be wasted on people who aren't interested in you.

> *"Even individuals need to develop a brand for themselves... whatever your area of expertise, you can take steps to make people think of YOU when they think of your field."*
> **Accelepoint Webzine**

2. Target Audience = Inside Knowledge

You can more easily keep your finger on the pulse of a niche market. Like the cat waiting outside the mouse-hole, by the time your target arrives, you are already set up. If you can stay one step ahead, you can begin looking for new target markets before yours starts dwindling.

3. Target Audience = Privileged Status

Another benefit of having a strong target market is that you can get under the skin of your people. You should know what their concerns are, what they are thinking. You can keep them close and communicate in many formal and informal ways. I know bankers, accountants and lawyers extremely well, which means I know their issues and I know where they hurt. If I was 'all things to all people', I would not be able to go this deep.

4. Target Audience = Deeper Relationships

With a clearly defined market for your products, your services and your influence, you can make a lasting commitment to client service. I call this 'going deep'. You can get to know less people more deeply with strong Client Experience Management (CEM) systems and procedures that make them loyal, make them obedient and make them take notice.

Enhancing Your Reputation Through Multiple Niches

If you can specialise in one of the four niche areas discussed earlier, you will stand a much stronger chance of creating a great reputation. Do you want your reputation to be built around somebody who delivers a particular thing, someone who delivers in a particular way, somebody who delivers to a particular crowd or someone who delivers to a particular region? You can go deep and you can focus your marketing and your reputation efforts like a laser beam.

Now it's time to imagine what your reputation might be like if you created a niche in ALL FOUR AREAS! The progression in your **pleasure**, your **prosperity** and your **popularity** is directly linked by your courage and laser-beam focus to specialise. It looks like this:

1. **No niche** = a weak reputation (generalist)
2. **Single-niche** = an 'okay' reputation
3. **Double-niche** = a good reputation
4. **Triple-niche** = a very good reputation!
5. **Quad-niche** = an awesome and unbelievable reputation as the ultimate 'go to' professional!

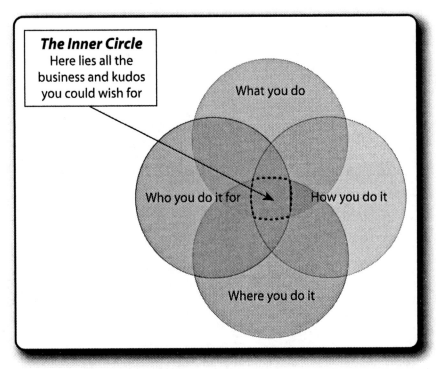

© Rob Brown 2007   www.thetripsystem.com

I am developing a 'quad-niche' with my speaking business. First, I only offer expertise on relationship marketing (which comprises business networking, reputation building and referral generation). These are all tightly focused areas around my **TRIP System®– Turning Relationships into Profits**. Second, I only deliver this material in two ways – keynote conference speaking and in-depth, long term development programmes. Third, I specialise in professional services – financial and legal professionals. Finally, I aim to do 90% of my business in the East Midlands of the UK.

How does this work out for me? Well, first of all, if you asked me to do some presentation skills work for you, or to speak on leadership, I could do it, but I choose not to. So I'd politely say 'no' and perhaps recommend you to a good professional who could. That's niching. And when someone asks me the difference between what I do and what my competitors do, I can easily explain how I go much deeper with the material and can deliver more targeted results. You could tell your clients and contacts what I tell mine - that it allows me to understand more intimately the needs and issues with a particular segment of business. It's in and around that segment that you're going to develop your reputation.

You also might ask me to deliver a one-off workshop for your team. I would probably say no, because it is only through my long-term programmes that I can guarantee sustainable change instead of short-term impact. Finally, you might ask me to speak internationally, and I'd probably say no.

Now before you think, 'Well, I don't have that luxury' or 'It's okay for you', let me explain how I say 'no', and when I might say 'yes'. First, if it's a 'no', I do my best to introduce them to someone who can give them a 'yes'. This could be a contact, fellow speaker or colleague. This is why it's important for you to build up your network of trusted colleagues, suppliers, advisers and providers that you can pass on leads, referrals and recommendations to. As these people start to know your speciality and your desire to work in particular niches, they would hopefully refer back to you the kind of work you're really passionate about.

Second, I will say 'yes' if the audience or client is right, the opportunity is right or the fee is right. In other words, you could take on something outside your core areas if you like it, you want to help somebody, it's interesting work, the fee is right and there is an opportunity for ongoing work and referrals. Otherwise, PASS IT ON! Saying no to things can be frightening and also liberating! It does take a certain amount of bravery and focus, but the rewards can be huge.

Can you have more than one niche? Yes, you can. But you have to be clever because there are three rules you must abide by:

The Three Golden Rules of 'Multiple Niching'

1. **Be Tight or Remote.** Keep your niches very close together (under an umbrella of some larger offering) or very far apart (so there are no conflicts).

2. **Be Flexible.** Recognise you'll probably need different marketing strategies for each. Remember you can't be all things to all people. You may have to market one at a time.

3. **Be Strategic.** Don't 'multiple-niche' for the sake of it. There has to be a clear benefit to this kind of strategy. Top US development guru Nido Qubein calls this 'intentional congruence'. Your areas of specialty should hang together well and compliment each other. If one of your specialisms isn't going well, consider that it may just need more time or better marketing.

Example 1

My mentor and one of the UK's leading motivational speakers, Nigel Risner[10], niches his audiences in three areas - housing associations, pharmaceutical companies and HR functions. There was no reason for this other than this was how his business developed. As you get known in an area of specialism, more and more people tend to take you deeper and deeper into it.

Example 2

Janet, a corporate relationship banking manager, already had a job-defined niche of working with companies turning over in excess of £3m. She decided she would niche in two areas – nursing homes and private schools. In the following year, her business doubled because all of her referral sources knew exactly what she was looking for. And as soon as any contacts came up in that area, guess who they called?

Example 3

One of the UK's best speakers on persuasion is Philip Hesketh. He runs his business in two parts of the world – England and New Zealand. These two geographical niches work really well - he spends one particular month of the year with his Kiwi contacts and clients. "It's the only way I've ever been able to change the English weather in February!" he says. See www.heskethtalking.com

When you know who you are going after, it makes it much easier to market your products and services. Defining your area of specialty doesn't mean that you are saying 'no' to *every other niche*. It just means that you are getting yourself known in your specific target niche. There is no doubt you will attract people from outside your niche as your reputation becomes stronger and more prolific. But you will always have the choice to say 'no' or to say 'yes'!

> *"It's choice not chance that determines your destiny."*
> **Jean Nidetch,** founder of Weight Watchers

What to Do if You Don't Have a Niche

Let's look for a moment at what you can do if you want more business or a greater profile but…

1. You've got no 'stand out' speciality area
2. You're new in a role and want to hit your targets sooner rather than later
3. Your client portfolio is too wide-ranging to pick out any definable group
4. You're young and relatively inexperienced
5. You've got too many areas of specialisation and you're struggling to 'pick a lane'.

Here's what you can do. Over a period of three to six months, see as many clients or customers as possible. Remember that your customers could be your colleagues or your line manager – anyone that benefits from a service you provide and is in some way responsible for rewarding you for it. Then ask yourself any or all of the following questions:

1. Who were your most lucrative?
2. Who did you love working with?
3. Who did you relate to the most?
4. What products or services, if any, were most 'in demand'?
5. What products or services did I most enjoy delivering?
6. Was there any particular method of delivery that was more satisfying or lucrative than any other?
7. Were there any geographical areas with a large concentration of your clients or customers?
8. Can you define a geographical radius in which you'd like to work?
9. Might this area be lucrative enough if you market it right?
10. Is there an identifiable niche you can market to?
11. Is there enough work in this niche to build your business?
12. Is anyone else working this target market?

These questions will help you snip around the edges of your core offering and trim down what is probably a hotchpotch of offerings, methods, locations, contacts, clients/customers and connections. Remember it takes courage to begin narrowing down a target market, and there comes with that a sense of liberation. You should also bear in mind three things as you go through these exercises:

1. You actually don't have to define every niche to build your reputation. It is important you niche, but if you can't nail one down, there are four principal areas to choose from, remember? These are what you do, how you do it, where you do it or who you do it for. Once you define one niche, others could become apparent later.

2. Just because you choose to go after a particular audience, doesn't mean you can't say 'yes' if something 'off your radar' approaches you. For instance, a great lead/prospect/referral could fall into your lap and if it fits, by all means take it. It just means you don't go chasing these kinds of leads and you don't go marketing to them.

3. When looking at specialist niches and target audiences, many people start with a product or service first and then look for people to fulfil that need. It is sometimes more effective to start with the end in mind. Build what they need and they will come!

> *"Be a generalist, but market yourself as a specialist. Know who you are, and know how you are different from anybody else."*
> **Howard Shenson**, consulting guru

You need a deliberate strategy to help you understand all you can about the niches available to you. Once you know that, you can begin to clearly define the value you provide, figure out how to match it to your target audience and minimise or remove those parts of your service or product that are 'value neutral' or 'value negative'.

Now you've dug deep. You've either uncovered or confirmed who you are. You've gone some way to deciding how you want to position yourself. You've also given a lot of thought to possible specialist areas in the four main niches. You're getting close to defining the reputation you want and then sharpening your tools to make it happen!

Defining Your Reputation

You are not yet at the building stage. To build the reputation you want, you have first to define it. You now know what a reputation is, you know where your strengths lie and you know what, if any, niches you'd ideally like to operate in.

You now need to put everything together and come up with a Unique Value Proposition (UVP) that encapsulates what reputation you would like to build. Your UVP begins to explain the difference you would like to make. It is traditionally a business development tool aimed at your target market. But, with the help of your friends, family, colleagues and contacts, you can also use this exercise to help define the reputation you want. This is about getting people to buy you as much as buying your products and services.

This is all about positioning yourself in your marketplace. Your UVP is similar to but a little more involved than your USP (Unique Selling Proposition), and aims to help your target market answer these questions:

1. **Why should I work or partner with YOU, as opposed to someone else who offers the same thing you do?**

2. **When I need something that you provide, why should I choose you, above and beyond all my other choices, including the choice to do nothing?**

3. **What value, what results, what solutions and what relief can you bring to my life, my business, my problems and my pain that I cannot get anywhere else?**

These all amount to the same thing: **why you and not your competition?** By articulating answers to the above three questions, you lay the groundwork for your UVP. This then represents your opening gambit in networking situations, and the start of all the good rumours you want others to spread about you! It helps people distinguish you from your competition.

The best way to generate real attraction and education with your UVP is by weaving in more value. People need to know where you add value. 'Adding Value' is a common buzz phrase in business today. Understanding the essential elements and finer distinctions of adding and creating value is the key to success.

What does 'value' actually mean? Why is everybody saying you must add value? The dictionary states that **value is worth, desirability or money well spent.** For you, that means you must know your value, price your value and sell your value. Unless you know what value you offer, it's hard for you to sell who you are and what you do.

If you can articulate this consistently and with clarity, you are well on your way to shaping the reputation you want. A word of caution though, value is often twinned with the phrase 'value for money'. If you compete on price, then your customers and clients are price conscious. To mix metaphors, they will 'screw you down to the ground until there is no wood left on your pencil.' When your competitors lower their price, you are going to lose out unless you do the same. So it makes sense to compete on value.

If you are struggling to articulate the value you provide or want to provide, or the difference you make or want to make, you will struggle to articulate what you want to be known for. The best way to articulate the value you offer is to ask the people who are supposed to be experiencing that value. This is almost like a satisfaction questionnaire, but it is no longer acceptable to be merely satisfying expectations. You need to exceed expected value.

> *"Customer satisfaction is worthless, customer loyalty is priceless."*
> **Jeffrey Gitomer**[11], author of The Sales Bible

Asking a client if they are satisfied will not make a lifetime client. There are better questions. Here are some examples of ways to ask your clients Value Seeking Questions (VSQ):

Intro:
"Julie, I am asking all my clients to see how I can serve them more. Once I establish this, it will also help me gain more successful clients just like you. I am doing this exercise with all my clients. Will you take a moment to answer some of the following questions?"

1. *"What are the three most important ways that you have benefited from our working together?"* (Accept what they say, and then press for clarity/simplicity/truth.)

2. *"In what surprising ways have you benefited, perhaps outside of what you pay me to do for you?"* (Press for truth/openness.)

3. *"Is there an area of our work together that you would like to spend more time on?"* (Be patient as they create this; this tells you what they want more of, and may help you expand your client list by serving others with similar needs.)

4. *"If we were meeting here five years from now, what has to have happened by then for you to be happy both personally and professionally with the work we have done together?"* (Be patient as they process this.)

As well as helping you articulate your UVP, VSQs have many advantages:

1. Benchmarking. Once you know what value you are giving, you can systemise it and look to exceed it on a consistent and regular basis.

2. Advocacy. When you ask a VSQ, you can help your client internalise this value. Once they recognise and understand the value you offer, they are more likely to become lifetime clients. You are making them aware of what they are getting which differentiates you from others. This is your Unique Value Proposition and it makes them advocates. That means they tell others about you and spread the word.

3. Loyalty. Once your clients know and appreciate the value you are giving, it will be harder for them to go to a competitor. Those key areas that press your clients' buttons will facilitate meaningful differentiation and thereafter greater loyalty and profitability. And of course, you can also use this value to attract other value-conscious clients.

> *"Lack of loyalty is one of the major sources of failure in every walk of life."*
> **Napoleon Hill**, one of the earliest authors of the modern genre of personal success literature (1883-1970)

When you ask great questions of your best clients, you can find out what value means to them. If you do this right, then two things will happen. First, when your name comes up, people will immediately think with the utmost clarity about exactly what you do and why you are the best. Second, when a need for your product or service arises, you will be the first name that comes into people's heads.

You should now be in a position to answer some or all of the following questions:

1. Which of your unique attributes are going to help you stand out and click with your target audience?
2. What, above all else, marks you out from the crowd?
3. If you haven't got anything, what could it be?
4. What do you offer that adds distinctive, remarkable, measurable value?
5. What makes you different from all the rest?

6. What separates you from them?
7. Is your unique differentiator what you offer, or the way you deliver it?
8. Are you unique in the way you target what you offer at a specific group of people?
9. Is there something about your personality, your personal style or your business methods that marks you as different?
10. Can you do something different to what everyone else is doing?
11. What makes them all the same?
12. Can you create your own category?
13. How do you enrich people's lives?
14. How can people benefit from working with you, knowing you and being with you?
15. What is it about you that is special?
16. What can you offer that few other people can?
17. What can you make happen for people and situations?
18. What do you find easy that other people find difficult?

Crafting your UVP is putting in a few sentences what you want to be known for. If you cannot articulate this yourself, how do you expect others to talk and think about you in the way you want them to? You must be able to state in unequivocal and benefit-laden terms the distinct nature of your offering. This could be:

- *The unique or specialised value, knowledge or results you offer*
- *The unique, specialised or excellent way you work*
- *The specialised market, industry or demographic you really know inside out.*

In other words, where do you really make a difference? If you can encapsulate this in a few sentences or even a few words, you make it easier to market yourself, to get known, to get hired and to be spoken about. This is what I call the 'Fewer Than 10%'. It refers to the fact that fewer than 10% of the population achieve real success in their chosen career. If you want to be part of this small group of successful people, ask yourself the questions in the 'Fewer' illustration below. If the answer to any of these questions is 'no', do all you can to change them into 'yes'. If you are successful in all these areas, you will begin to stand out from the crowd.

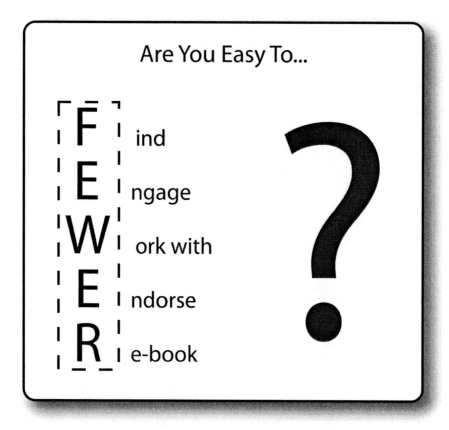

But, to be unique, you do not necessarily have to be the best, the fastest, the most knowledgeable or even the most high-profile. But you do need to distinguish yourself from the crowd in some way. You have to find a way to be 'front of mind'. You have to become the number one choice and the 'go to' professional, and that means differentiating yourself in some special way.

It is useful here to note what doesn't work in a UVP. *30 years in business is not always a unique differentiator, because other people may have that same attribute.* You can say things like…

'We give quality service'

'We've been around a long time'

'Our products are guaranteed'

'We're REALLY hard-working'

'We put the customer first'

'We'll get the job done'

… but everyone is saying things like that. These are generalities that will give you a 'so what?' or a 'who cares?' answer, if you are lucky. Most of the time, people will not even hear you. Your UVP is in many ways your **Elevator Speech**. It's that 30-second commercial or introductory message that you could deliver to somebody in the lift or elevator when they ask you what you do. It's that short, succinct answer that gets over what you do in a matter of seconds. Put another way, this label is:

- Your introduction or 'audio logo'
- The critical point that can make or break your business relationships
- The most effective way you've got of getting over what you do and how you do it
- Your first impression, and possibly your last
- Your one big moment to impress or depress, depending on what you say and how you deliver
- A brief 'statement of intent' on how you help people
- A simple phrase that captures the fundamental value you bring to your clients
- A catch-all 'tag-line' that conveys what you do and what makes you special
- A conversation prompter that sparks interest in you and your services.

The mechanisms by which you define your UVP may be similar to those exercises in earlier chapters where you explored your unique character and what makes you tick. Brainstorming with a few colleagues, friends or clients may help you distil your uniqueness, the benefits you offer, the credibility you have and the reason why people should choose you.

> "A strong, precise USP [UVP] will act like radar, targeted at the right prospects for your offering. There are certain clients you want, and equally important, certain clients you don't want. Far too many people engage in shotgun marketing, desperately seeking every client they can get. The problem is that this is not very profitable. Your particular situation, your business strong suits and

> *specialised experience make what you have to offer much more valuable to certain prospects than to others. Creating your USP requires being aware of your strengths and weaknesses and those of your competitors. It requires a lot of open-minded creativity on your part. Copying someone else's will simply put you back in the pack with everyone else. Your business is unique and your USP should also be unique."*
>
> **Elsom and Mark Eldridge[12], authors of**
> 'How to Position Yourself as the Obvious Expert'

To begin articulating your UVP, compose a short phrase that sums up who you are, what you do, what makes you special/sets you apart and how that unique quality makes you uniquely fit for your target audience. Your phrase does not have to be elegantly worded. It is a statement to help you stay focused. It's not your sales pitch. Keep it to one paragraph if you can. This may include such elements as who you are, what you do, who you do it for and what sets you apart.

If you want impact with this, include benefits for your target audience which accrue when they work with you. Think about what is different to your competitors and possibly has a real 'wow' factor. This will begin to give you your personal identity – the expression of who you are and what you do that is unique.

Depending on your role and your speciality, your final stage may be to consider coming up with a snappy slogan that encapsulates all the elements of your offering. This takes time. It will communicate not just about meeting your client's needs. It's about meeting their needs in a way that is distinctive and different from your competitors. If you cannot find this difference, you will find it hard to compete on value and may be in danger of becoming a price-based commodity. Do your clients really see you as different to your closest competitors? If so, ask yourself how and why? What can you do to make your UVP more distinctive and appealing?

Another consideration in refining your UVP is your rivals. It's important you check out the competition and take a good look around at your competitors. If you want to leave the pack behind, you need to know who is running alongside you.

The Role of Your Competitors in Building Your Reputation

It doesn't matter whether you're looking for more business, more money, more attention or more recognition, you need to know who you're fighting against. *You need to know your enemies.* You have to find out who delivers similar services, both in other companies/ sectors/industries and in your own. You need to identify who else is after your clients/customers. You need to know who they are and what they are saying to your target audience. As I often say to my clients:

> *"If what you do is optional or has competitors, you have to market yourself. You must differentiate yourself. You must give people a reason to choose you, above and beyond all of their other choices, including the choice to do nothing."*

So think about who your competitors are. Who's opposite you across the table? Who are you running alongside? They could be the people sitting next to you in your office or the rival business down the road. Look back at the goals you set and your ultimate ambition. *This is where you will find the competition - along the road you want to be on.* They are ahead of you as well as beside you.

There are **five** reasons why you should keep an eye on your competition:

1. **You gain a better understanding of what they are doing to compete with you**

2. **You gain fresh ideas about how you can improve your own brand and service**

3. **It helps you to benchmark your offering and to structure negotiations and proposals better**

4. **It keeps you motivated to continually improve what you do**

5. **It gives you information for new stories, case studies, marketing channels and content for your materials.**

Take a close look at your rivals and make a list of what they offer. What are *their* reputations? What do their testimonials tell you? What do people say about them? Most importantly, what are they *failing* to offer? What are they missing that you can provide? Depending on exactly who your competition are, here are **five** ways you might be able to monitor what they are getting up to:

1. **Subscribe to your rivals' newsletters.** You can either do this through a non-specific email address (like hotmail) or ask someone else to do it for you. You might not want them to know you're a subscriber, and they might not want you to be.

2. **Check out their products and literature.** What are they asserting and claiming, and what are they illustrating and demonstrating? Who are they marketing to and how are they doing it? Might it be worth you buying some of their products or services? Getting close to them anonymously is not a bad idea.

3. **See them perform.** It's not always possible, but if they give seminars, clinics or presentations, can you get yourself in the audience, or at least send someone else along to spy on your behalf? You can always learn things, even if it's how 'not' to do something. You could also go to internal/ external networking events, seminars and conferences where you know they will be. Then you can see first hand who they talk to and who they know.

4. **Probe your contacts and clients.** When you ask others about your competitors, you get the inside scoop on where to defend and where to attack. It also helps you to innovate and improve on anything you see working well.

5. **Bookmark them.** Sounds obvious, but few people do it. Create a favourites list of your competitors' websites. When you come across new competitors add them to the list. Websites are now a major shop window for every professional. You need to know what's in theirs. You

can also monitor their movements. This sounds a little devious, but it's actually all legal and practical! This kind of tracking is an advanced way of keeping ahead of the game. There are many (free) and ethical internet tools you can use to find out when people change content on their website, what keywords and phrases they are using, track their rankings, who runs their company and who holds the trademarks they are using.

The trick is not to become too absorbed with this. Sometimes it can be quite intimidating when your rivals seem to be way ahead of you in certain areas. You are not doing this to get despondent. It's good if you're behind them in a way – you've got more ways you can improve and they won't take too much notice of you! You are doing this to draw level and hopefully pull away. You need to have a healthy awareness - not a morbid obsession. You must stay close to your target market.

> *"When we stopped focusing on our competitors and started focusing on our customers, that strongly became number one."*
> **Sir Terence Leahy**, CEO of the
> UK's leading supermarket, Tesco

Geoffrey Moore[13] states that a value proposition should answer the questions: "Why should I buy this product or service?" as well as "Why should I do anything at all?" It is a clear and specific statement about the tangible benefits of an offering. He gives a template for creating a value proposition, which may be referred to as a positioning statement. Note the first portion of the value proposition asserts the value of the offering and the second sentence asserts the positioning of that value.

First Sentence:
- For [target customer] who [statement of the need or opportunity], the [product/service name] is a [product/service category] that [statement of benefit].

Second Sentence:
- Unlike [primary competitive alternative], our product/ service [statement of primary differentiation].

As an example, if I run my TRIP System® offering through this template, it looks like this:

For *financial and legal professionals*
who *want to win more business and create more opportunities*
the TRIP System®
is a *members-only website*
that *offers a complete relationship marketing resource of articles, educational materials and development programmes.*

Unlike *other marketing resources,*
my service *concentrates specifically on Turning Relationships into Profits, whether profit for you is more money, more influence, more attention or more recognition.*

How might that work for your offering?

Now you have taken a healthy look at the competition, you're positioned, you're clear on what you want to be known for and you've established your UVP. Your final consideration is deciding why you want the reputation you do. In other words, what are your reputation goals?

What are Your Reputation Goals?
....

You've sorted out who you are, what you're offering and to whom. Now you must look at where you're going. To develop a reputation, you need to decide what you really want out of life, who you really want to be and what you really want to be known for. You need to know where you're going and what your career, your business and your life will look like when you arrive.

All personal goals can be categorised into what you want to be, do and have. And that order of outcomes is important. If you want to **have** certain things (possessions, opportunities, riches) then you need to **do** certain things. If you need to **do** certain things (network better, sell more, speak more confidently, win more business) then you need to **be** certain things. It all comes back to your character.

As an example, if you want to complete a marathon, you must do certain things (train diligently - run hundreds of miles to prepare). In order to do those things, you have to become a certain kind of person. You have to be someone who sticks to their goal, someone who is driven, motivated and persistent. Your ultimate success will come through the cold mornings, through the temptations to do other things and through the inclination not to train if you don't feel like it. And that comes from inner character. Your inner beliefs and values will drive you forward through any tough times, any moments of doubt and any external criticism.

Your goals will help you decide how to prioritise and focus your efforts. For instance, if you wanted your reputation to bring you more fame than fortune, you might go about it differently. You'd have a different strategy for developing more business than you would for more recognition. There are three possible **Reputation Goals**, depending on what you want your reputation to do. Every single outcome can be accommodated by one or more of these goals.

Pleasure

This is simply peace of mind. If your **Reputation Goals** are aimed at bringing you more happiness, fulfilment and engagement with life, then you will need to craft a **Pleasure Reputation** accordingly.

> *"Pleasure is the object, duty and goal of all rational creatures."*
> **Voltaire**, French author and philosopher (1694–1778)

Prosperity

While prosperity brings a certain peace of mind, a **Prosperity Reputation** is more about 'having' than 'being'. It brings you material, tangible benefits that you can see, feel and measure. It's about money, riches, possessions, status symbols and income.

> *"There is nothing wrong with men possessing riches. The wrong comes when riches possess men."*
> **Billy Graham** (American evangelist, b.1918)

Popularity

If you want your reputation to be such that it makes you something of a celebrity, someone who turns heads and a person people take notice of, then you are looking for a **Popularity Reputation**. To put it simply – you want to be famous! Your strategy for this is in some ways complex (because the 'fans' you want are often fickle creatures) and in some ways easy (you only have to look at some of the 'from nowhere' celebrities around to see how that could happen).

Plenty of people seek this kind of reputation. This is the most fickle of reputations to both build and sustain. It's the one that can be most easily faked – and easily 'uncovered'.

> *"We are so vain that we even care for the opinions of those we don't care for."*
> **Marie Von Ebner Eschenbach**, Austria's greatest 19th century female author (1830-1916)

To help you decide what you want from your reputation, tick any of the boxes in the grid following that appeal to you. Whichever column has the most ticks represents your **Primary Reputation Goal.** This gives you your most significant reason for 'raising your game', and will dictate how you go about it.

129

Primary Reputation Goal Grid

PLEASURE		PROSPERITY		PROFILE	
Contentment		Assets		Love	
Passion		Wealth		Adulation	
Enjoyment		Money		Popularity	
Time		Income		Status	
Space		Riches		Admiration	
Peace		Bonuses		Acknowledgement	
Happiness		Commissions		Fame	
Fulfilment		Referrals		Reverence	
Challenge		Sales		Approval	
Excitement		Business		Attention	
Satisfaction		Clients		Recognition	
Purpose		Security		Respect	
Direction		Material Possessions		Acclamation	
Interesting Projects		Holidays		Trophies	
Career Options		Rewards		Appreciation	
Attractive Ventures		Perks		Esteem	
Interesting Opportunities		Privileges		Awards	
Add up your totals here					

Now it's likely you'll have ticks in all three columns. The key questions for you are:

1. **In which columns do you have the most ticks?**
2. **What Reputation Goal, if you achieved it, would probably give you the most satisfaction?**
3. **If you could only have one Reputation Goal, which one might it be?**

Once you have decided on your Reputation Goal, you can begin laying down your personal strategy for building the reputation you want, which will bring you the outcomes you desire.

You should, by now, be able to complete these two phrases:

I want to be known for/known as _____

_____.

If I achieve it, it will mean/the benefits to me will be _____

_____.

If you can do that, you've got the motives and the blueprint.

You're ready to build!

Section 3: BUILDING REPUTATIONS

You've already come a long way. You have stripped away your outer packaging and gone some way to discovering who you really are and what makes you tick. You may even have dug deep on who you really want to be in this life and what you want to be known for. Let's just recap on exactly what you've done to get to this point. You've come through five steps:

1. **Understanding.** You now know exactly what a reputation is. It's the *Reason Everyone Pays* you money, attention and respect. It comes from within - you build your reputation on your beliefs, your values and your character.

2. **Motivation.** You now understand why you need a reputation. Without a strong 'reason why', you will not take the action you need to make the difference you want to make. You saw how you have to exploit the *Ten Universal Laws of 21st Century Business*. You now know what a good reputation will do for you and how fragile it can be.

3. **Foundation.** You have explored some of the tools you have to work with – your character, your values, your strengths, your passions and your skills. You did some exercises, conducted some research and had some conversations to confirm or discover who you are, deep inside. *You've done 'introspection'!*

4. **Definition.** You have begun to define the reputation you want. You've considered selecting a target audience, choosing one or multiple niches and perhaps crafting your *Unique Value Proposition.* This clearly states what you want to be known for. You've got to decide on your reputation (if you haven't already), maintain it (if you have it already), claim it (if you should be there already), or become it (if you're not there already).

5. **Direction.** You've set out your Reputation Goals. These fall into three categories – *Pleasure, Prosperity or Popularity.* This helps you decide what you want most from your reputation and why.

Now all you have to do is devise your personal reputation plan and execute that plan!

Creating Your Personal Reputation Plan

If you want a reputation that reaches further and more powerfully towards the people you want to influence, you need to plan carefully and build diligently. This is a step-by-step process.

> *"Rome was not built in a day."*
> **Ovid,** Roman poet (43BC-17AD)

There are ten strategies to get yourself known for the right things. Not nine, not eleven, but ten. Every which way you can build your reputation comes under one or more of these ten. *Your strongest and quickest route to the reputation you want is to use a combination of a few.* One will be slow and two will be more than twice as fast. Ten might not be so effective if you're diluting your efforts.

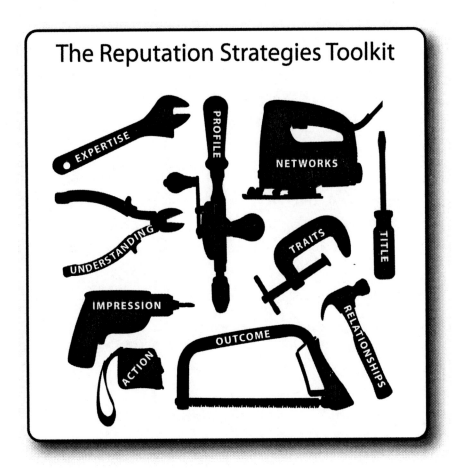

Now let's look at each of these in turn as you decide how you're going to make that reputation happen!

Reputation by Relationships

This is where you make use of who you know, namely individuals, associates and contacts. You can easily see that people judge you on the basis of the company you keep. If you get around 'good people', you'll be seen as one of the 'good people'. Achievement guru Brian Tracy uses the phrase 'scratch with the turkeys or fly with the eagles'. If you want to build your public perception by this route you need **Reputation by Relationships**. Another name might be **Reputation by Association**.

As you will see later, building your reputation this way is similar to **Reputation by Profile**. The key difference is that profiling is getting known. It's them knowing you. Relationships in this context are all about you knowing them. It's who you know.

Dictionaries describe the word 'relationships' like this:

- *A state of connectedness between people (especially an emotional connection)*

- *A particular type of connection existing between people related to, or having dealings with, each other.*

From a business and personal perspective, all of your relationships go through three basic levels: knowing, liking and trusting. In many ways, this is a numbers game, because you can guarantee that if 100 people know you, not all of them will like you. This is not because you are not nice or likeable. This is simply because some people just don't connect, don't click, are not on each other's wavelength and are never meant to like each other.

Moreover, if 100 people like you, not all of them will trust you. This is not because you are untrustworthy or because you lack credibility. This is simply because some people are naturally suspicious, untrusting or wary.

> *"Trust is the hardest thing to find and the easiest thing to lose."*
> **Anon**

The numbers game applies, because the more people you want to like you, the more people you need to know you. And the more people you want to trust you, the more people you need to like you. Networking is a fantastic way to meet these people and build up these numbers.

Everyone you're connected to is a reflection of you, your choices, your values and your reputation. People like people who are like themselves, so others have a right to judge you by who you associate with. People are also attracted to people who are either like them, or like who they want to be. So your relationships and associations reflect not just who you are, but where your intentions lie and the kind of person you want to become.

If you want to build your **Reputation by Relationships**, you have to look at *two key groups*:

1. **The people you associate with now**
2. **The people you associate with in the future.**

137

The former group are, in part, responsible for your *current* reputation. The latter group will help create the reputation you want down the line.

In the short term, you really need to look at who you're getting around and spending time with. Your family and relatives are a unique case, because you largely cannot choose them. It's cruel to say you're stuck with them, but the good news is that, in most cases, they have a very small effect on your reputation. Who you are at home is not generally as influential to your external reputation as who you are when you do what you do. Everyone is mortal in their own house!

Externally, if it turns out you have contacts and associations that are (at worst) holding you back and (at best) not taking you any further forward, it may mean a 'culling' of sorts. That's a ruthless way of saying 'get rid'. You can do this gently by phasing them out over time, or more brutally by cutting ties, switching allegiances and severing the cord.

It is said that people are either radiators (they give off energy) or drains (they siphon energy out of people). They are positive or negative. They lighten up a room when they walk in or lighten up a room when they leave. Can do or can't do. Enabling or hindering. Possibility people or obstacle people. It goes without saying that you ought to be in the former groups if you want to build your **Reputation by Relationships**.

Let's say you've identified that to get where you want to be in your public perception, it means you need to change who you want to be seen with. To cultivate new networks, contacts and associations, there are three stages you go through.

1. WHO. You need to identify the (kind of) people you want to be seen with, next to, alongside, around, in front of and behind. Think in terms of individuals rather than companies. It's easier to target if you have real people in mind. These could be clients or customers, contacts, mentors, role models, key influencers, leaders or 'up and coming' movers and shakers. If you can't get to them immediately, think about who is close to your target associations.

 One of the people I'd like to get alongside is singer Robbie Williams. Not because I have illusions of performing on stage with him, but because an associate and I have written a song that would be perfect for him to record. And I'd like to put that song in his hands! So I'm constantly asking people two questions: 'Do you know Robbie Williams?' and 'Do you know anyone who knows Robbie Williams?' I figure that writing a song for Robbie Williams wouldn't do my reputation or my bank balance any harm at all!

Think who you'd like to be mentioned in the same breath as. Think of who you'd like to name drop. Think of who you'd like to meet. Think of who you'd like to know and be known by. Think of whose mobile phone number you'd like to get. Think of who you'd like to have a conversation with. Ultimately, think of who you'd like a relationship with. If you can learn from them, benefit from their presence in your life, accelerate your development with them, create opportunities from them and work with them, then these should be on your 'virtual board of directors'.

2. WHY. If you're going to approach these people, you have to do a little research. Learn about them. Get familiar with the way they work. Read books, listen and pay attention to what they've written, said or recorded. Get on the internet, work your network and ask one of the great all-time questions – **'Who do you know who...?'**

Find out what they think, what they believe, what they like and don't like. Understand what drives them, what they're passionate about, what they struggle with and what they really want. This tells you where they're hurting. Make sure you know where they're heading, what their goals are, what their legacy will be and what they need to get there.

You do all this for three reasons:

1. When you meet them, you don't want to appear ignorant or a stranger.

2. You need to find out if you're making the right choice – sometimes people you put on a pedestal are not quite what and who you think they are when you finally get alongside them. A little due diligence may save you a lot of heartache and wasted time.

3. You must know where they're hurting, what they need, what their Achilles' heel is. You must go in with an offer, a suggestion and a good opening gambit. You must make them curious, interested, engaged and wanting to take

140

things forward. It really helps your reputation if you can entice them into your life as well as ingratiate yourself into theirs.

3. HOW. Begin befriending these people. Find out where they go, where they play, where they work, where they relax and who they know. Find out who knows them. Ask around. Mention them by name. Get networking. Get writing. Get asking. Get on invitation lists and databases. Turn up on purpose or by accident. You've probably heard of the 'six degrees of separation'? It states that whoever you want to meet, you're never more than six handshakes away from them. It's just a case of getting yourself connected. Go as high as you can. Sometimes networks function on horizontal levels – so you need to get above the canopies of the forest before you can see the sunset.

One technique to get close to someone is to pay for access. Some gurus and mentors have 'inner circles' where you pay a few thousand just to get close to them. The more money you spend, the closer you get! This is usually money well-spent if you've identified this person as someone you really want to get around. Even at ground level, by joining their club, buying some of their products or services or making some basic connection, you sow a seed that can grow into something bigger.

Another way to build relationships with and get closer to key people is to offer them something. Find out where they're hurting and relieve them of their pain. Even the top people in the top organisations have problems that need solving. If you can position yourself as the antidote, the solution and the answer to prayer, you have a shot.

> *"Everything about business comes down to PEOPLE. Where in business can we escape the impact of human care, human creativity, human commitment, human frustration, and human despair? There is no reason for anything in business to exist if it does not serve the needs of people."*
> **Bruce Cryer**, Vice President of HeartMath LLC in 'Re-engineering the Human System'

Yet another way to find and connect with people is by reaching them online. Do they have blogs, websites, online articles or online networking profiles? There are lots of terrific networking organisations out there, and lots of places to access all the information you need.

If you're not such a people person, the next strategy might be the one for you.

Reputation by Expertise

This is where you become known and famous for what you can do. This could be **skills,** which are the things you have been taught or learned or acquired, or **talents** – attributes and abilities you were born with. *Skills are what you give yourself. Talents are what God gives you.*

> *"Everybody has talent, it's just a matter of moving around until you've discovered what it is."*
> **George Lucas**, director of Star Wars

This is probably the most common route to positioning yourself in the shop window of desirability and exclusivity. Not so long ago, expertise was equated with the number of years you were in business, or the degree/diploma that hung on your wall. That has changed: people are now more interested in the results you can produce than in whether your career started 25 years ago, or whether your degree is from a major university.

Everything else being equal, the person who can position themselves as an expert will be more sought-after, win more business with less effort, command higher fees, be approached by the media for their opinion and be more recognised as the 'go to' professional for their key discipline.

When you can position yourself as the number one expert, you put yourself in line to receive the biggest rewards. You don't have to be appointed by anyone other than yourself to become an expert in your field. If you can deliver to your prospects' unique needs, people will be interested in you, no matter how brief your business experience or how few diplomas grace your walls. Becoming an expert takes work, but it's within your reach. You don't need a special degree, but you do need a willingness to learn.

Your expertise will also be the foundation of a strong business that delivers great service. This will generate word-of-mouth referrals that attract clients with less effort because you have proved that you deliver results that people seek, want, and need.

Remember it is not as important to be the expert as to be seen as the expert. So assuming you're already pretty good at what you

143

do, you need to be looking at ways to convince others of your expertise. Later in this section, there is a comprehensive list of reputation-building techniques. For now, any strategy that gets you in front of the right audience or wins you credibility with that audience is viable if you want to leverage your expertise. So think radio, TV, magazines, online sites, books, teaching, speaking, seminars, blogs, third party endorsements and testimonials.

When you utilise these media, remember that the best way to leverage your expertise is to focus on distinct target markets you can realistically hope to dominate. Why? Because market niches are above all, manageable. You can get your mind around them effectively enough to design a marketing strategy that speaks in personal terms to real prospects. And from earlier chapters, you already know the importance and benefits of specialising.

As an example, you'll recall how I work mostly with banking, financial and legal professionals. They are similar enough, with similar challenges, so I can speak into their situation with authority and expertise. In other sectors I would struggle to have the same credibility. It also means I can market them very specifically rather than running after every chicken in the pen and catching none.

Get good and get known' is the phrase that pays if you want to build your **Reputation by Expertise**.

And what is an expert? Someone who does their best at all times, who learns as much as possible, who becomes the most brilliant, most clever, most wise and most knowledgeable person on the planet, in one area of knowledge and work.

Reputation by Profile

This strategy simply means you raise your name and your game by getting yourself out there! It means you become ubiquitous, omnipresent and prolific.

Here is a powerful visual way of seeing what you need to do to develop a reputation. I adapted it from an idea by top speaker and marketing consultant John Timperley[14]. I call it the **Relationship Pyramid,** or sometimes the **Profile Pyramid**.

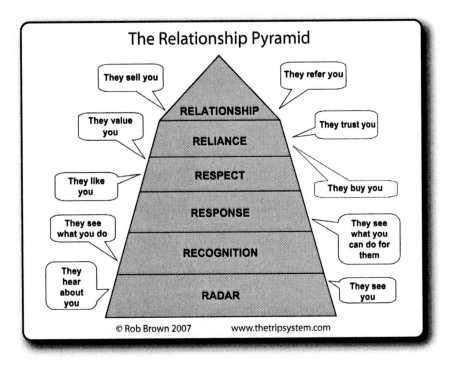

If you want to be known, you have to raise your profile. If you want to be known by certain people you have to get on their radar. There are six levels on the Relationship Pyramid, pictured above, that you have to attain before you can say you really know someone

145

and they know you. The objective is simple - move people up the Pyramid. The higher up they go, the more likely they are to buy from you, listen to you and even sell for you. Let's look at each of these in turn.

Level 1 - RADAR

This is making sure people see you, 'clock you' and acknowledge you. It is the spark that starts relationships and begins the long-term process of turning strangers into friends and suspects into prospects and clients into evangelists on your behalf.

Think about it. There are only five ways you can come across someone. Everyone you've ever met will fall into these five categories:

- Phone
- Face-to-face
- Correspondence (letter/fax)
- Reputation (you hear about them, read about them or see/hear them on TV/radio)
- Internet (email/blogs/websites).

You cannot get someone on your radar any other way.

Each level has two sides – people you know and people who know you. You want to be on other people's radars, and you also want certain people to be on yours. Both are important in building your reputation and your business. And if this is a numbers game, then the question becomes... how do you get people on your radar? Put another way, how do you start to know and be known?

Here are a number of ideas to raise your profile and kick your radar into gear:

1. **Volunteer for projects and causes**
2. **Join boards, committees and associations**
3. **Attend regular networking events**
4. **Get out of your comfort zone and introduce yourself to more people in existing situations**
5. **Write articles for local and trade magazines**
6. **Speak publicly**
7. **Get off your backside and out of your office!**

By doing these, you will see and be seen. But it's not enough to get you a reputation. You need to be recognised.

Level 2 – RECOGNITION

This is where people see what you do. The 'what do you do' question is guaranteed to come up early in your conversations. People want to fit you into their world. They want to know what you do and how you do it. They want to know if they can buy from you and use your services. More importantly, they want to know if they can sell to you and help you. And you want to know the same about them.

It doesn't take much of a conversation to communicate to people what you do. A great 'elevator speech' or 30 second introduction should accomplish this within the first few minutes of someone appearing on your radar. To move people up the pyramid to Recognition, you have to educate them on what you are offering. Please note - it is not enough to tell them what you do. They must see it and understand it.

147

Remember that if people cannot buy FROM you and cannot sell TO you, they have one remaining unanswered question. Who can they refer you to? In other words, who do they know that could benefit from your services? This makes what you say much more important, because you are not just telling somebody what you do. You are teaching them how to tell others what you do. That's when you know you have truly been 'recognised'.

The measure of how well you have introduced yourself, and how well people understand what you do, comes in how well they can repeat what you tell them to others. Next time you are networking, ask somebody else to introduce you and say what you do. If they struggle, you've got a job to do!

Once you've been recognised, you are looking for some kind of response. You want them to do something as a result of seeing what you do. Bring on the next level.

Level 3 – RESPONSE

This is where people see what you can do FOR THEM. This is where people begin to fit you into their life. They ask themselves what problems they have that you could solve and what pain they have that you could alleviate.

When people move to the Response level, they are interested in you. They start comparing you to their incumbents. They begin stacking you up against their existing providers, suppliers and advisers. They compare and contrast. And if you measure up, they bring you into their network. You join their team on the substitute's bench. You become the 'spare' when the wheel falls off their wagon. You potentially move onto their Preferred Supplier List.

It is very rare that they will engage you immediately, because they will either be using someone else to do what you do, be doing it themselves or simply not have an immediate need. But the great thing about the Response stage is that when people need what you do, you become 'front of mind'. At this early stage in your relationship, this is as much as you can hope for. Anything more is a bonus.

The way to move to Response is to ask great questions to uncover deeper needs. Think about four or five high-quality questions that you can ask somebody that may uncover a need for your particular area of expertise. If you can weave a few of these into your business conversations, you will evoke the right Response.

Once you have some kind of response, you have engaged people. This starts to develop respect.

Level 4 – RESPECT

This level is a quantum leap where people start to look at you in a personal way. This is where they like you and they respect you. Both of these create a powerful foundation for trust. If they have not bought your products or services at this point, they have certainly bought your arguments, your excuses, your opinions, your values or your advice.

> *"Probably no greater honour can come to any man than the respect of his colleagues."*
> **Cary Grant,** film star (1904-1986)

> *"If you want to command respect, you need to do four things: Have the wisdom to know the right thing to do in any circumstance, the integrity to do the right thing, the character to stand up to people who don't do the right thing and the courage to stop people who won't do the right thing. If you can do that, you'll command respect and people will beat a path to your door."*
> **Mark Goulston**, specialist in applied emotional intelligence and author of 'Get Out of Your Own Way at Work'

You'll learn more about the power of liking in **Reputation by Impression** later in this book. It is a key stepping stone to the attention, respect and money you want people to pay you. As for respect, well, let's see what that will do for you.

> *"Respect (n) ~ a feeling of admiration for someone because of their qualities or achievements; due regard for the feelings or rights of others."*
> **Oxford English Dictionary**

They start to give you credit and preferential treatment. They start to think not 'can they use you?' but '*how* can they use you?' At this level, things are really starting to happen. Now you need them to engage you with commitment. You want them to buy.

> *"Relationships cause people to want to be with you, but respect causes them to want to be empowered by you."*
> **John C Maxwell**, best-selling author, Christian minister and leadership expert

Level 5 – RELIANCE

This is where they buy you for real, principally for three reasons. They trust you, they rate you and they need you. If they already have an existing provider of your services, I call this 'the switch point.' They want to do business, and given the right timing, budget and circumstances, you're the one they'll come to.

Now this may mean they buy just a small part of you or your service, or invest a small amount of money in what you do. It's not that they don't want more of you. It's just that it's the 'right idea, wrong time'. Or 'right person, wrong time.'

When you move to some kind of reliance, you begin to establish yourself on their Preferred Supplier List. You begin to develop 'go to' status. They trust you and they depend on you. You can begin to market, advise and suggest on the back of your relationship and good name. Now you just need them to market for you, which means moving to the ultimate level.

Level 6 – RELATIONSHIP

This is the Holy Grail of the Pyramid! This is where people become your virtual sales force, your evangelists, your advocates, your story tellers, your word-of-mouth marketing arm and your fans. These are people that you have a real bond with. You can talk to them for ten minutes about nothing to do with business. You can call many of them friends. They don't just buy you, they sell you. They don't just rely on you, they refer you.

> *"Coming together is a beginning, keeping together is progress, and working together is success."*
> **Henry Ford**, pioneer US vehicle manufacturer (1863-1947)

You get people to the switch point and beyond by being ubiquitous. That means by being everywhere - by being in their face in a nice way. Think about reminding them you're around and open to do business. Think how you can help them by offering advice, help, contacts and even referrals. And that's before they've given you anything. This way you begin to convince them that a relationship with you would be good for them. *The ultimate way to move to this level is to build a relationship outside the transaction. In other words, be nice to them before you sell to them!*

If you want to raise your profile, you have to get talked about positively in as wide a circle as possible. That way, your name hopefully comes first into people's minds when they think of your area of work. This is called being 'front of mind' or sometimes 'top of mind'.

You can do this by networking, blogging, speaking, writing, and connecting. You do this by being a presence, by sticking around, by investing in relationships and networks long term. You do this with good propaganda. Get people talking about you. Generate good PR and make sure you pop up in the right places. *When you're everywhere, you're prolific!*

If you are in an employed position, you might also consider this Pyramid from an internal standpoint. Think of your colleagues and other departments within the company *as well as* your external connections with fellow professionals, prospects, contacts, customers and clients. Not all of them will rise to the top of the pile and that's good. You'd have way too much business, way too much influence and way too much money. And you wouldn't want that, would you?

If you are a little more cerebral and less inclined to want to put yourself about, this next strategy might be perfect for you!

Reputation by Understanding

This should be your chosen strategy if you know a lot and can bring clarity to people's situations and thinking. Some people develop a terrific reputation for what's in their heads. *If you know a lot, you can be a lot.* Brains can be beautiful! You can't beat a good education, so they say.

This strategy is similar to expertise, except that expertise implies something different to just knowledge. It has an element of 'doing'. Understanding is merely what you know – your knowledge, the information you hold in your head and the depth to which you can go with a particular topic. The difference is that when you know so much, you don't need to do so much. *People just come and drink from the fountain of knowledge!*

You gain a **Reputation by Understanding** if you devote yourself almost single-mindedly to the pursuit of specific subjects, ideas or topics. Gurus, sages, authorities and mentors exude this aura of understanding. They know stuff. They know how to do stuff. They have the ability to answer your questions and even answer the questions you can't even think of. They have deep knowledge. They study extensively. They go deep. *They are wise and they specialise.*

153

Gone are the days when you could be an expert on a range of subjects – there is simply too much knowledge around.

If you have a passion for personal development, for learning, for courses, books, seminars, manuals and mentors, then you could become known for your knowledge.

> *"If money is your hope for independence you will never have it. The only real security that a man will have in this world is a reserve of knowledge, experience and ability."*
> **Henry Ford,** pioneer US vehicle manufacturer (1863-1947)

How you leverage this kind of reputation is a different matter. Einstein said that information is not knowledge, implying that you've got to do something with it rather than just have it sat there. It used to be that people who developed a reputation for understanding generally looked for profile rather than profit from their efforts.

Now things have changed, and there is profit to be made from knowledge. One of the ways you can exploit this kind of reputation is in information marketing. There are many wise people on the internet peddling their knowledge in the form of books, e-books, online learning courses, educational materials and membership websites. Heavens, I'm one of them!

People will pay you for your knowledge. People will pay to get inside your head if you know stuff they don't. People will pay for shortcuts. People will pay you to save them time. People will pay for you to tell them things in 30 minutes that it took you 30 years to learn. People will pay you to understand complex or wide-ranging topics and explain them in terms they can comprehend.

To develop your **Reputation by Understanding**, you need to be passionate about learning. You need to be inquisitive. You need to ask lots of questions. You need to search for answers. You need to be a sponge. You need to be a voracious reader. You need to live, breathe and eat your chosen subject. You need to attend seminars, conferences and workshops. You need to invest in your intellectual development. And then you need to put it in a format people can access and understand.

> *"The only thing standing between you-as-amateur and you-as-expert is **dedication**."*
> **Anon**

If you're not a brain-box, a scholar or a guru, there are other ways to develop a reputation. If you have more of an ego and crave a little bit of celebrity, this next strategy might become your favourite!

Reputation by Title

When you have a title, you create a name of importance, recognition and substance. This strategy leverages where you are in the grand scheme of things. Where you are in the pecking order dictates to some extent your reputation. Think about your position, your qualifications and your awards. When you have letters after your name, people begin taking you a little more seriously.

If you want to earn your **Reputation by Title**, you could go *three* ways:

1. Academic. *Spend a few years and long nights studying for a solid qualification which will vouch for your expertise.* Degrees, PhDs, Masters, MBAs, Diplomas and Certificates all fit the bill. They can be awarded by educational establishments, governing bodies, professional organisations or trade associations.

Such credentials add credibility, standing and authority to your reputation. They say to people:

- *"I can do this – I've studied it from 50 different angles and could write you a thesis on it!"*
- *"You can trust me here – I've spent years diligently analysing problems for such a time as this!"*
- *"There's no need to worry about my commitment to your cause. I've sacrificed my personal and private life and applied myself diligently and single-mindedly to this subject, so this is a piece of cake!"*

2. Role Specific. *Work yourself into a role or job title which elevates your reputation.* The higher up or more prestigious your position is in your organisation, the more it says you're good and worthy. The more it says you're promoted and elevated, hopefully on merit, the more it tells people you're *the special one* and *the important one.*

156

When you walk into a room as the Director, Manager, CEO, Chairman, Principal, Chief, Boss, Executive, Instructor, Leader, Lecturer or Teacher, your reputation goes before you. You get respect and deference. People are more amiable, compliant and polite. People are happy and even privileged to do things for you. People are honoured and even thrilled to meet you.

If you can work your way up to any kind of management or leadership status, you can achieve **Reputation by Title**. If you can generate some kind of title of your own, it can add a layer of credibility which can earn you extra respect and attention. Why do you think people try to buy peerages and aristocratic titles?

3. The Golden Envelope. The third and final way you can use this strategy is through awards and accolades. Think seriously about entering competitions, running for awards and putting yourself forward for prizes. Few people actually go for these. And even if you don't win, you can use phrases like 'runner up', 'nominee' and 'short-listed for'.

The reason these strategies work is that these titles, qualifications and accolades are largely earned and bestowed. They give you added credibility because they're not just names, they're third party endorsements. Depending on the reputation you want to build, they can be very effective.

 Conference speaker Amanda Clarke[15] runs Optimum Training, the UK's leading first aid training company. This is what she puts on her email signatures underneath her contact details:

Amanda Clarke, MCIPD, M Inst D, CPVA,
CPBA Managing Director
2004 Cheshire Women in Business Award
Winner
2004 Institute of Directors Cheshire Director of
the Year Award Nominee
2003 Business Insider Magazine - 42 under 42
Award
2002 HSE/TASC report "the best manual,
training and infrastructure I have ever seen"
1999 Daily Telegraph Small Business Award
Runner up - Best Business Growth through
Technology

Do you think she has a certain reputation? Do you think
you could trust her with your audience? Do you think
she might know what she's talking about? You bet! And
she's not got those for herself – she's been given them and
she's earned them.

Reputation by Actions

Some reputations are made in an instant. During the September 11th attacks, Mayor Rudolph Guiliano made something of a name for himself. Already a controversial but largely popular figure for his zero-tolerance stance which decimated the New York crime wave, his place in history was assured when the Twin Towers were hit. He showed incredible standards of inspired leadership in rallying the city and galvanising the emergency services.

He was a man who gained his **Reputation by Actions**. Building a reputation this way is usually easier if you're in a position of leadership. You influence people by what you do. When you walk the walk, when you perform, when you execute, when you do good and great things, you develop **Reputation by Actions**.

This strategy needs an audience. Action needs to be seen before it's talked about. It needs a medium for expression. People need to view and interpret your actions favourably. Once they do, they'll possibly share that with others. There's a chance you'll be talked about in good terms.

Reputation by Actions *is also affected by timing - it matters when you strike.* Certain events, crises, trends or critical moments can bring out actions and reactions in you that you never knew were in there. Although Guiliano already had a certain reputation, it was elevated dramatically by the events of 9/11.

To exploit this strategy, you can do certain newsworthy things (row across the Atlantic like motivational speaker and adventurer Debra Searle[16]), you can lead or manage in a particular way (Jack Welch of GE built his reputation largely on his management style), or you can manufacture the circumstances that reveal those particular behaviours you want people to see. You can win gold medals, climb big mountains or endure through great adversity. All of these will bring you a reputation through your actions.

All of that said, this strategy can be something of a reactive game. This next strategy might be more within your control.

Reputation by Traits

If you want to develop your **Reputation by Traits**, you need to understand the difference between character and personality:

Your Character – those values and beliefs you cling to and hold dear. Examples are integrity, honesty and compassion. You can develop these over time and they are shaped as much by circumstances as genetics.

> *"Character is what you are in the dark."*
> **Dwight L Moody,** famous US preacher (1837-1899)

Your Personality - those distinctive personal qualities and attributes you were born with. This describes how creative, academic or practical you are. It describes whether you are gentle or aggressive, introvert or extrovert, loud or quiet, driven or laid-back, optimistic or pessimistic, risk-taking or cautious, selfless or selfish. These are not easy to change. They are inborn. They are an indispensable part of you.

Both character and personality will influence your behaviour, which is the outward expression of them both. When you add them together, they make up a very unique you!

In 1936, two researchers (Allport and Odbert) found 17,953 words to describe the ways people are psychologically different from each other (e.g. shy, trustworthy, laconic, phlegmatic, kind, conscientious, anxious...). All these words describe personality traits.

160

Traits are distinguishing qualities or characteristics of a person. Traits are a readiness to think or act in a similar fashion in response to a variety of different stimuli or situations. They seldom vary - once you have them, you have them. But occasionally, changes can be made. For instance, studies show that women tend to become more dominant, independent, and self-confident over time.

Another researcher, behavioural scientist Raymond Bernard Cattell (1905-1988), narrowed this listing of 17,000+ words down to 4,500 words and then narrowed these down further to 171 trait names, and finally down to 16 personality factors in 1949. See the table on the next page. Other researchers have come up with different factors and even narrowed the list down to five common traits.

But however we try to classify them, the point is that there are thousands of shades in between the extremes in these personality traits. *That is why everybody is unique.* And that is why your personal brand is personal, because only you have your blend of qualities and talents, and only you have that distinctive set of values and characteristics which make you the person you are.

How does this affect your reputation? Well, your reputation is simply people's opinion of you. Once people make up their minds, it is very difficult to change them. This can be very good for you if you can create a strong initial impression. First thoughts are like a jelly - they set very quickly. Otherwise, you will be one of those 'slow burn' people that make a negative or neutral first impression but of whom people say, 'He/she really grows on you over time.'

Cattell's 16 Personality Factors

1. Reserved v. Warm

2. Concrete Reasoning v. Abstract Reasoning

3. Reactive v. Emotionally Stable

4. Deferential v. Dominant

5. Serious v. Lively

6. Expedient v. Rule-Conscious

7. Shy v. Socially Bold

8. Utilitarian v. Sensitive

9. Trusting v. Vigilant

10. Practical v. Imaginative

11. Forthright v. Private

12. Self-Assured v. Apprehensive

13. Traditional v. Open-To-Change

14. Group-Oriented v. Self-Reliant

15. Tolerates Disorder v. Perfectionist

16. Relaxed v. Tense

Research shows that you like people who are similar to you. In basic terms, you like people who are just like yourself. The similarity can be in the area of opinions, personality traits, background or lifestyle. If you want to build your **Reputation by Traits**, you have to exhibit qualities that people find attractive and appealing.

> *"To be successful, you have to be able to relate to people; they have to be satisfied with your personality to be able to do business with you and to build a relationship with mutual trust."*
> **George Ross,** Executive Vice President and Senior Counsel, the Trump Organisation

If you have negative traits that upset people or put them off or make you awkward to deal with, you will find it difficult to create a positive reputation. If you have great qualities, play on them! Make them a part of your message and your personal brand. People interpret your personal brand in a way that makes them say and think certain things. This becomes your reputation.

Examples of a negative Reputation by Traits:
- George has a really bad temper
- Julie is really moody
- Jim is never open to a good idea
- Jenny is so messy
- Will is so disorganised
- Jimmy is too loud
- Dave talks too much

Examples of a positive Reputation by Traits:
- Ali is very creative
- Mindy is really clever

- Alan can turn his hand to anything
- Norman is really conscientious
- Dave is a really good listener
- Andy really has the 'gift of the gab'
- Georgia is really caring
- Kate is the most helpful woman I know

Examples of a neutral Reputation by Traits (can be interpreted both ways):

- Madison is a real maverick
- Amanda is a very careful driver
- Clive is a real joker
- Marjorie is totally unique
- You can trust Jimmy to come up with the craziest ideas.

So what do you want people to be saying about you? You can only control what they say, do and think when you control yourself.

> *"Ask yourself, 'How will my reaction reflect on my business reputation?' before responding to any situation. The more dramatic the situation, the more critical your response will be."*
> **Jimmie Wilkins**, director of Chemeketa Small Business Development Center, Oregon

Sometimes our personality traits are hard to change and equally hard to control. If you're looking for as much control as possible over your reputation, this next strategy might be the one for you.

Reputation by Impression

Out of all of the strategies for building your reputation, it's this one that allows you the most latitude in being distinctive and unique. This strategy involves how you come across to people. It encapsulates your stature, your aura, your physique, your image, your looks and your interactions.

You probably know that once people make up their minds, it is very difficult to change them. *Part of developing a good reputation is making people remember you* – in a positive way – from the outset. It makes you come to mind when people need something that you do. It's making people think of you when they receive all kinds of cues and triggers.

How does **Reputation by Impression** work? Well, the bad news is that part of this is genetic.

- If you're tall and imposing or small and petite, you'll probably create a more lasting impression than if you're of average height. Think of Arnold Schwarzenegger or Danny de Vito.

- If you're clinically obese, you may be more memorable than if you are of average weight. Think of Pavarotti or soul singer Barry White. White's wonderful voice aside, he became known for his 'larger than life' image.

- If you're extremely attractive, you'll be more easily noticed and remembered. Think of movie stars and models. Think of pop stars and pin ups. Elle MacPherson, Caprice and Claudia Schiffer are wonderful people, I'm sure. But they've made their reputation on their looks and their bodies. Research shows that (however unfairly and without even thinking) you judge good-looking people as being more talented, kinder, more honest and more intelligent than others. This is especially so in recruitment situations. The message here is to make the best use of your persuasive skills, thank your parents, take good care of yourself and make the best of what the good Lord has given you.

- If you're extremely distinctive in your look, you'll also be more easily noticed and remembered. With his shock of wild grey hair, Einstein had a certain look. His face is one of the most recognised in the world.

If you're short on genetics and Mother Nature has not blessed you with any such physical attributes, here is the good news! You can influence your look with the way you dress, the way you groom and the way you look after yourself. Think of pop stars Pete Burns, Boy George and Marilyn Manson. That might not be your style, but it's certainly memorable!

Think of icons who go for a certain look. Richard Branson has a very casual image that is nonconformist and very relaxed. Simon Woodroffe is a top UK entrepreneur, star of 'The Dragon's Den' TV series and founder of Yo! Sushi. You'll rarely see him without a very colourful pair of shoes with his suits.

This strategy lends itself well to extremes. If you're 'out there', you'll be remembered. Business people who wear bright socks or colourful ties are making a statement. It makes them stand out because it creates an impression. Some people only wear clothes of a certain style or colour. I bet you know someone who you've never seen without a tie on! Some people become known for their accessories. Whether it's perhaps, scarves, tyres, badges, shoes, belts, glasses or jewellery, you can make a statement with just about everything that adorns you.

You can shock, you can surprise, you can swim against the tide and you can break with convention. Not wearing a tie is a reason to be remembered if you walk in circles where ties are the norm. You could have a catchphrase, a feature, a gesture, even an affliction which you can use to create a personal brand that will get people talking.

Building your **Reputation by Impression** works best if your chief reputation goal is **Popularity**. It won't necessarily or directly bring you the other two – **Prosperity** and **Pleasure**. They may come as a consequence. But this is about fame, celebrity, recognition and differentiation. It gives people a reason to talk about you, which is a fantastic start for any reputation!

However, beyond the larger than life image, the coloured socks, the fancy hats and the loud ties, you need something of substance to ensure your brand endures. This is why celebrities come and go. This is why today's eccentric is the strange 'has-been' of tomorrow. You need something meaningful and real to go with the 'fluff'.

The final dimension of this strategy is with your interactions. This describes the way you connect with people. It's the way you treat people, talk to people, talk about people and behave with people. Here are the best eight ways to attract and interact to create an 'interactional' **Reputation by Impression:**

1. **Use People's Names.** *People love hearing their own name.* Not excessively, but considerately. Dale Carnegie, author of 'How to Win Friends and Influence People', wrote that someone's name is the sweetest thing they will ever hear. That doesn't mean over-using someone's name. It just means making more of an effort with names and using them astutely and warmly. It makes a good impression!

 From the Royal Navy's elite Submarine Service to the World Memory Championships to building a company that has taught over half a million people how to learn, Michael Tipper's[17] interactive, entertaining and empowering style shows that learning, achievement in business and success in life are simply a matter of belief. Michael is a good friend and is someone who uses more of his brain than most humans! He recognises the power of names in building relationships – he says it is one of the best things you can use your memory for. And as a world memory champion, he should know!

2. **Be Co-operative.** *Think help, not sell.* When you have a giving attitude, you connect by wondering how you can help and what you can do for someone, rather than what you can sell and what they can do for you. Bottom line,

competition tends to lead to hostility, while co-operation tends to lead to positive feelings and mutual liking. You only need to look at the classic 'good cop - bad cop' routine to see this in action. When you concentrate on giving first and gaining second, people will find you attractive and magnetic. People will want to be around you. People will talk about you and want to help you in return. People will endorse you, and can refer you and 'big you up'!

3. **Be Likeable.** *The dictionary describes liking as a regard or fondness for something.* A big slice of the 'liking pie' is down to good interpersonal skills. Study upon study has revealed that people with strong verbal skills are more influential and convincing and are perceived as having more competence and credibility. There are lots of things you can do and say to be liked by more people. It's almost certain that you prefer to say 'yes' to the requests of people you know, like and trust. In short, liking equals agreement. If you say the right things in the right way, you can make almost anybody like you more easily, more deeply and more quickly. Be polite, respectful and sincere. Never forget words like 'please', 'thank you' and 'excuse me'. Let people know that you appreciate their time and effort. Make sure every customer, client, supplier or general public contact is a pleasurable experience for them. Remember: 'The customer may not always be right – but they are always the customer'! Be honest and upfront in all communications – this can earn you lifelong relationships with your clients and business associates. If you have staff,

make sure they do exactly the same in all their dealings with people.

> "The main work of a trial attorney is
> to make a jury like his client."
> **Clarence Darrow,** famous lawyer and leading member
> of the American Civil Liberties Union (1857-1938)

 Ever heard of the Greatest Salesman in the World? Joel Girard has been called the world's greatest car salesman by the Guinness Book of World Records. He became extremely rich selling Chevrolets from the showroom floor in Detroit. For twelve consecutive years, he was the number one car salesman, averaging more than five cars and trucks sold every day he worked. This was incredible by any standards. When asked about the secrets to his success, he said it was simply giving people two things: a fair price and someone they liked to buy from. "Put them both together and you get a deal," he said. If you want to be more influential and persuasive, it is absolutely crucial that you get people to like you.

4. **Be Engaging.** *Look to make contact with people.* Be aware of opportunities for 'random connections', 'divine appointments' and 'chance encounters'. You can make a personal connection with just about anybody at just about any time in just about any place. All things being equal, research suggests you are attracted to things that are familiar to you. If you 'click with chemistry' it's possible

to make almost anybody like you, want to listen to you, understand what you are about, appreciate what you can offer, and want to start a relationship with you on almost any level. Be interested and people will think you are interesting. Be fascinated and people will think you are fascinating.

> *"When dealing with people, remember you are not dealing with creatures of logic, but with creatures of emotion; creatures bristling with prejudice and motivated by pride and vanity."*
> **Dale Carnegie**, author of
> 'How to Win Friends and Influence People'

5. **Be Around.** *There has been a lot of research done on the role of familiarity in relationships and its impact on attraction and magnetism.* Familiarity affects magnetism because your attitude towards something is influenced by the number of times you have been exposed to it in the past. In other words, contact and connection improve liking. When you think about it, all relationships are built this way. Strangers turn into friends through prolonged contact and interaction. So go and turn some strangers into friends!

6. **Be Positive.** *People are more attracted to upbeat, optimistic, positive and passionate people.* If you are motivated, you will be motivating. When you are happy, it makes other people happy. When the dog wags its tail, it makes other dogs wag their tails. When you smile, you make other

people smile. Research shows the way people feel about you is influenced by what you are associated with. One experiment showed that people dislike weather reporters more when the weather is bad than when the sun is shining! Be positive and associate yourself with positive things, people, products and services. That's why people like people who like the same football team. Positive people are attracted to positive people. Make the link between you and good, positive energy.

> *"Always be positive and energetic. Never say you are too tired or too busy. It gives people the impression that you cannot take on more work, more clients or more projects."*
> **Penny Power**, founder of online networking organisation Ecademy

7. **Be Passionate.** *There is nothing as attractive as someone who loves doing what they do.* And there is nothing as unattractive as someone who hates what they are doing. So love what you do. There are so many people in jobs that they are well-trained to do, but if they don't enjoy their work, these jobs are unlikely to bring out the best in their talents. If you want to draw people to you, get yourself known and make yourself an attractive proposition, don't be scared to show a little passion and enthusiasm!

8. **Be Deliberate.** *This could be called living your life on purpose.* When you are doing what you were born to do, you start to become very attractive. Leading wealth

consultant Roger Hamilton calls this 'being in your flow'. Top UK motivational speaker Clive Gott[18] often reminds his audiences that 'when you are on fire with desire, people will come from miles around to see you burn!' To do this, you need to be engaged in what you were born to do. You need to be doing things that float your boat. Things that excite you and engage you. If you think about what you would do even if you didn't get paid, this is being deliberate. If you think about what you would spend your time on if money were no object, then this is your purpose. When you live on purpose, you create an attraction and a magnetism that makes you irresistible and creates an awesome reputation!

You are the one key differentiator between you and everybody else in the whole world. Being distinctive in the way you look, come across or interact with people is an excellent way to create a reputation that counts. Still, if that's not your style and you're more about results than image and interaction, then this next strategy could be your prime directive.

Reputation by Outcomes

This method is all about what you make happen. It's about results, end-products and solutions. It is similar to **Reputation by Expertise**, but different in that the strategy focuses very much on the end rather than the means.

If you hit your sales targets, you will develop a **Reputation by Outcomes**. Few people will be concerned about how you do that.

They will be more impressed by the end result. Typical outcomes you could build your name on could be:

- Turning around a really bad situation
- Overcoming a major challenge or obstacle
- Hitting or surpassing a challenging target
- Achieving an excellent Balanced Scorecard
- Submitting a particular project before or on deadline
- Completing a specific task in an impressive way
- Achieving a particular promotion
- Passing a rigorous test with credit
- Devising a new system, process or product
- Creating something new and innovative
- Achieving a particular result
- Making the grade
- Performing outstandingly
- Winning!

There are times when you'll see an opportunity to do something really special for someone. When you do, the ripples of your 'pebble in the pond' can earn you a name and a reputation.

However, if you really want to build your **Reputation by Outcomes**, you have to be ready for failure too. You have to perform, and all performances are subject to both subjective and objective judgments, a range of success criteria and elements of risk. The chances are that the measurement of your success is governed by factors outside your control. Targets and pass marks and grades may well be set by others and not yourself.

Nonetheless, if you love the adrenaline and the buzz of performing, and the satisfaction and adulation of achievement, then this may be a key strategy for you in developing a reputation.

 Nathan is the number one sales professional in the UK division of one of the world's largest pharmaceutical companies. Last year he was number three. He has doubled his salary in that time. He has enhanced his reputation to such an extent that the company are now offering him a number of key positions as well as paying for his MBA studies. As long as Nathan is working ethically and professionally, his company are much more concerned with his results and his sales than his methods and systems. They are more concerned with outcomes than expertise. Nathan knows this and he plays the game.

There are some caveats to using this strategy. The more tests you pass, targets you hit and obstacles you conquer, the more people will expect. Unless you jump off the treadmill, more will be expected. Of course, the rewards will be great, but you cannot be too disappointed if you're expected to do significantly more than your colleagues and rivals.

This is good in a way, because it makes you 'up your game'. But it can be exhausting and relentless. It is a good short-term strategy, but ultimately unsustainable in the long-term. You can blaze a trail today, but tomorrow it might just be a dirt track. And no matter how hungry you are, there will always be somebody hungrier, leaner and more mercenary who wants the accolades and the results more than you do.

Reputation by Networks

You should see by now that if your reputation is good, it will win you business, loyalty and options. You will derive pleasure, make profit and earn profile. You can become the obvious expert, and revel in the wealth, the status, the power and the influence it brings you!

The tenth and final strategy to make this happen is **Reputation by Networks**. This is similar to **Reputation by Relationships**, except that it does not focus on *who you can influence* and specific individuals but on *where you have influence*. This includes associations, government, decision makers, clubs, organisations, royalty, aristocracy, panels and boards.

If you want to build your **Reputation by Networks**, you need to be 'a player'. You need to be 'in the game'. You need to be moving in the right circles. You need the right memberships and the right associations. You need privilege, access, shortcuts, inroads, backstage passes and invitations.

While many of these things come as a result of having a great reputation, you can become very famous simply by turning up, volunteering, being put forward, endorsed and invited. Once you are privy to this level of networking, you gain access to all kinds of opportunities, information and leverage.

There are many ordinary people who develop an extraordinary reputation through their networks. This strategy, coupled with **Reputation by Profile**, is one of the most potent ways to get known for the right things by the right people. Here are the seven best ways to build your **Reputation by Networks**:

1. **Solicit Invitations to as Many Events as You Can.** You may not be able to attend them all, but you can cherry pick the best ones to achieve your reputation goals. With discretion, politeness and respect, you can also build excellent relationships with event organisers and hosts. This will stand you in good stead for the future.

2. **Look Out for Networking Hubs.** Hubs are people who sit in the centre of great networks. Hubs are people who know what is going on. Hubs are the movers and shakers. Hubs are the key players. Hubs know 'who's who and what's what'. Befriend them. Ask their advice. Go where they go. See if you can also introduce them to networks that they would like to break into. It will not be long before you become a networking hub yourself!

3. **Find a Networking Mentor.** This is somebody who has been where you're going. This is somebody who can open doors for you and introduce you to the right people and cut corners for you with the right networks. This is somebody who is really connected. Ask how you can help them and ask if they would be willing to help you.

4. **Join Up.** Membership tends to cost, and elite membership tends to cost even more. This is not including the social element. But if you want to win the lottery, you have to buy a ticket. You have to buy your way in and you have to put your money where you want your reputation to be.

There is nothing unethical about this. It is just the way it is. Hopefully the more you pay, the closer you get to the centre and to the elite.

5. **Volunteer for Projects, Assignments and Positions.** Once you have broken into a network, find out what committees and boards you might serve on. This is a fantastic way of building your **Reputation by Networks**. You become known very quickly and you are given responsibility and decision-making power very quickly. Because of the time commitments, fewer people than you would think step forward for such positions. And if there are no projects or assignments to sign up for, suggest some! With two or three well chosen networks, associations or clubs, you can develop a powerful and far-reaching reputation in a relatively short time.

6. **Start Your Own Club.** If you cannot join them, beat them! Every club, organisation, association and network started somewhere. More than likely it was started in the same way you will start yours - with two or three people having a good idea, shaking hands and making it happen. To start with, it will be small but perfectly formed. If you have spotted a niche audience that needs representation, a particular geographical location that needs serving, or a specific need that you can meet, you have the makings of something that others will want to join. With one or two key testimonials and endorsements from heavy hitters and influential personnel, you can make it happen.

7. **Become a Preferred Supplier.** If you can be or offer something that a particular network needs, you can come in through the backdoor. From the catering to the entertainments, you have a way in. From organising to speaking, there are ways you can break in that do not involve membership. Think about what expertise, what products and services those members and patrons might need. Then source it, supply it and milk it!

The Two Unspoken Reputation Strategies – Building Credibility and Trust

As well as the preceding ten core strategies for building your personal reputation, there is one that underpins them all – credibility. Your credibility is closely linked to your reputation – and is essential to it. Credibility sets you apart from your competitors and gives assurance to your clients, contacts, customers or employers. What does it mean? The dictionaries tell us that credibility is the quality, capability, or power to elicit belief. It's the believability of your words, deeds and motives, and to what degree people act on those.

Credibility works on three levels, and to develop a strong reputation, you must be effective in all three:

1. **Your personal credibility** – selling yourself, showing your personal expertise and speaking with authority.
2. **Your persuasion credibility** – selling your ideas, your arguments, your propositions, your opinions and even your excuses.

179

3. **Your company credibility** – selling the organisation that stands behind you.

Obviously, the stronger your expertise the stronger your credibility. But, assuming you are working on your expertise all the time anyway, what else can you do to boost your credibility?

The answer is to build trust. A combination of trust and expertise gives you the credibility that is vital to your reputation. Trust is a firm reliance on your integrity, ability, or character. There are plenty of experts and professionals out there who do not get the work and recognition they desire because they cannot be trusted. They may be liked and even admired, but when it comes to recommending them or hiring them, you're not too sure.

Here are six ways to ensure you make yourself easier and more likely to be trusted, and therefore enhance your reputation and credibility:

1. **Be reliable**. Do what you say you will do, when you say you will do it. Reliable people can generally be trusted. People don't want surprises. They want to be able to predict outcomes and rely on you to deliver. This also means being consistent. If, given a certain situation, you do one thing one day and something different the next, you become unpredictable and therefore less reliable.

2. **Be rational and logical**. People will trust you more if you are level-headed and make decisions based on reason rather than emotion. Again, people don't like surprises. As much as they may

appreciate your creativity and your eccentricities, they want you to conform to their expectations and norms. It builds trust.

3. **Be responsive**. People will trust you more if you respond well to their needs and concerns. A trust-inducing response is one that's timely, perceived as 'nobly motivated' (as opposed to self), helpful and appropriate, and will do your reputation no end of good.

4. **Be honest**. Integrity may sound like an old-fashioned word, but the truth is that it has never gone out of fashion. You can make short-term gains by overselling and exaggerating, and other dishonest practices, but a strong, long-term reputation is built on this old-fashioned value.

5. **Get around trusted, discerning people**. You have seen the power of **Reputation by Association** and you know that you reflect the company you keep. You will seem more trustworthy if you keep the company of respected individuals whose opinion, and practices, are valued and trusted. You become the benefactor of borrowed trust until such time as they trust you in your own right.

6. **Be candid**. People will trust you more if you point out the downside to your product or service. Don't make inflated claims. People are not likely to believe you if you tell them that yours (whatever it is) is the best. Promise less and deliver more. That way people's expectations are generally more than satisfied, and you put precious trust in the reputation bank.

If you are worried that being too honest and pointing out 'problems' might lose you business, there is a solution. *Point out a downside that you know won't worry your prospect.* Choose something that is not going to affect them or their decision to use you/purchase from you. That way you are letting them into your confidence, at no risk. Also, if you work for a company that takes a dim view of admitting weaknesses, it gives you a ready defence – that you shared something that you knew wasn't going to damage your client relationship. But you must weigh up the risks of this approach before deciding to take it.

The Role of Influence in Reputation

The more your reputation grows, the more influence you will have. Conversely, the greater your influence, the greater your reputation. So increasing your influence is another aspect of building your reputation, and one that weaves in and out of all of the ten strategies above.

So like the chicken and the egg, which comes first? Do you gain more influence in order to increase your reputation, or do you want a better reputation so you can be more influential? The truth is that these words can often be interchanged, and it's hard to have one without the other.

> *"Influence: the power or ability to affect someone's beliefs or actions."*
> **Compact Oxford English Dictionary**

The dictionaries describe personal influence as the power you wield (either knowingly or unknowingly) to affect people, things or events. They particularly emphasise that relaxed type of power that operates without any direct or apparent effort. This marks a key difference between influence and persuasion. Influence is something you have and happens with or without your involvement. Persuasion is something you do and can only happen with your effort.

Linking this to reputation, you can see that both are similar. Both make people do, say or think certain things. And the good news is that you are already an influencer. In all your dealings with other people, you do exert some kind of influence. The bad news is your influence can be negative. So finding the keys to *positive influence* is vital to building your reputation.

> *"Every man is a hero and an oracle to somebody, and to that person, whatever he says has an enhanced value."*
> **Ralph Waldo Emerson**, American author, poet and philosopher (1803-1882)

Whether you are cutting a deal, selling a product, managing a department or convincing a client – your success will depend largely on your ability to influence people.

So you need to ask yourself: *how much influence do I have right now with the people I want to be taking notice?* Whether it's low or high, there's always room for improvement. If it is low, this is an area you need to pay particular attention to.

One way of discerning your level of influence is to ask yourself this question: if you and several colleagues are given the same idea to share with me, who would I listen to? You must be clear here that you have different spheres of influence. If you ever think you have the same influence over everything and everyone, try bossing someone else's dog or children!

In his famous book, 'Becoming a Person of Influence', New York Times best-selling author John C. Maxwell[19] explains that there are four levels of influence: **Modelling, Motivating, Mentoring and Multiplying.**

I like to see this as a pyramid, where the number of people you influence decreases as you rise up, but the impact of your influence increases. As a musician, I often interpret this from a musical perspective!

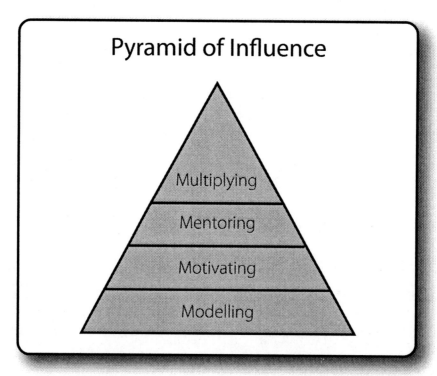

1. Modelling – Hearing Your Song. *At your first meeting, people are influenced by what they see and what they hear you say.* In music, the first impression you get of a song is when you hear it for the first time. You know how you immediately fall in love with some songs the moment you hear them? Your feet tap, your hips sway and you get 'bitten'! Even at this early stage, your life or work can begin to become a model for theirs – if they like what they see.

> *"Example is not the main thing in influencing others, it's the only thing."*
> **Albert Schweitzer,** German medical missionary, theologian, musician, philosopher and Nobel Peace Prize winner (1875-1965)

2. Motivating – Listening to Your Song. *The second level of influence is motivating others.* You achieve this when you begin to relate personally to people. In musical terms, this is the stage where people have not only heard your song, but have stopped what they are doing to listen to it. As you communicate and as they see you in action, you can meet not just on an intellectual level but an emotional level. This means that you can either encourage them or discourage them. If they don't agree with you or relate to you, your influence wanes. But if people make a connection with you, they can be positively motivated. And if your attitude is right, the relationship will build up their confidence and trust in you. Result? More influence.

3. Mentoring – Singing Your Song. *Mentoring is a higher level and more personal.* They see you as not just one of many people they admire, but as someone who they wish to emulate. In my musical analogy – they begin to sing your song. If you establish this closeness of relationship, you can literally change people's lives. It means a sacrifice of your time and energy, but as you help them reach new levels of achievement it can be extremely rewarding.

> *"A teacher affects eternity; he can never tell*
> *where his influence stops."*
> **Henry Brooks Adams**, American writer (1838-1918)

4. **Multiplying – Performing Your Song**. When you reach this stage, the person you are mentoring has learned so much from you that they are able to pass it on to others. It's like someone who enjoys singing your song so much that they are willing to perform it to others. So your influence is multiplying. Not many people reach this height of influence, as it involves long-term mentoring. This means you have to be very unselfish. It also benefits your reputation enormously.

It is good to remember that the higher your position in a company, or the more successful you become on your own, the greater responsibility you have towards others – as your influence will be great. You can change the world for better – or for worse!

> *"From everyone who has been given much, much will be*
> *demanded; and from the one who has been entrusted*
> *with much, much more will be asked."*
> **Jesus Christ,** Gospel of Luke, Chapter 12 verse 48
> (Holy Bible, New International Version)

Maxwell goes on to explain the ten essential qualities for people who want to be influential:

1. Have Integrity

Maxwell says that integrity is the quality most needed to succeed in business. Steven Covey, author of 'The Seven Habits of Highly Effective People', agrees: *"Even so-called good human relations techniques will be perceived as manipulative... if there is little or no trust, there is no foundation for personal success. Only basic goodness gives life to technique."*

2. Nurture Others

Exerting authority over others is not the key to influence – a caring attitude is. Every human being needs nurturing by someone – and if it's not by you, it will be by someone else who sees the value of it. And that other person will be gaining influence, not you. If you see the world as a dog-eat-dog competition, you will never nurture anyone, as you will see others only as enemies. You need to see others as possible allies in your journey to a high reputation.

One word of warning, though. Ensure you nurture qualities like independence and initiative in others – because if you don't, they can become dependent on you. If people become dependent on you, you are not helping their growth but hindering it. A nurturing person gives love, respect, security, recognition and encouragement. This kind of person is attractive, and if you are attractive, you will draw people into your sphere of influence.

> *"A life isn't significant except for its impact on other lives."*
> **Jackie Robinson,** US baseball player

3. Have Faith in People

If you work with colleagues or employ others, you need to win their support in order to succeed. The surest way to gain that support is by showing faith in people. Few people have someone who believes in them. If you step up and do just that, they will respond to you. If you teach people to have faith in themselves and tell them you believe in them, this gives you an advantage. Most other people will not be sending out these positive messages to your colleagues, employees or contacts. Affirmation is an incredibly powerful tool. But it must be genuine – most people can tell if it's phoney.

> *"Outstanding leaders go out of their way to boost the self-esteem of their personnel. If people believe in themselves, it's amazing what they can accomplish."*
> **Sam Walton,** Wal-Mart founder (1918-1992)

4. Listen to People

> *"To listen well is as powerful a means of influence as to talk well and is as essential to all true conversation."*
> **Chinese proverb**

Too many people who are ambitious to build their reputation are egotistical or have a superiority complex. In turn, this often makes them impervious to other people's views, and too fond of the sound of their own voice. Don't fall into the same trap. Influence is gained by listening to people, not ignoring them. Listening shows respect, strengthens friendships, increases the pool of knowledge and ideas, engenders loyalty and gives you greater insight into what is going on around you.

5. Understand People

Breakdown in relationships is a major cause of failure in business. If it happens to you, it is inconceivable that you will not lose some influence and damage your reputation to some extent. Such breakdowns are usually caused by not understanding people and how to work with them. If you can get on with people, you can succeed in almost any type of business. But arguments destroy business and prevent you climbing the ladder.

It is too easy to think that someone else is out to get us, just because they disagree.

> *"When we understand the other fellow's viewpoint –*
> *understand what he is trying to do – nine times*
> *out of ten he is trying to do right."*
> **Harry Truman,** Former US President

A course in psychology, personnel management or human resource development might be a good idea if you are struggling to get along with other people. If you need a little coaching here, remember that people are motivated by their needs. Reward them with what they want and you're onto something!

Basically, there are two different lines of thinking that help to pinpoint rewards and motivation. The first is people centred. Some people are influenced more by the need for internal rewards, and others more by the need for external rewards. Internal rewards are things like a sense of accomplishment, self-esteem or fulfilment. External rewards are things like money, recognition, status symbols or public praise. Choose the right rewards for the right people, if you want to cut any ice with them.

The second is situation centred. Brought down to a very basic level, every action is motivated by the need to get away from something (pain motivation) or the need to move towards something (pleasure motivation).

> *"Nature has placed mankind under the governance of two sovereign masters: pain, and pleasure. It is for them alone to point out what we ought to do, as well as to determine what we shall do."*
> **Jeremy Bentham,** author of 'Principles of Morals and Legislation', 1879

When you are motivated by pleasure, it will bring you pleasant feelings or experiences such as elation, ecstasy, delight, joy and enjoyment. Examples are that you work hard so that you can go on holiday three times a year, or to provide a certain standard of living for those you care about.

As you would imagine, pain motivation brings about an avoidance of unpleasant feelings or experiences such as aches, irritations, anxiety, anguish, chagrin, discomfort, despair, grief, depression, guilt, regret and remorse. Examples are that you work hard so you won't be in debt, or to ensure your loved ones avoid a certain standard of living that would be unacceptable to you.

A basic understanding of what motivates certain people to do certain things can help you be more influential and therefore enhance your reputation with that person in that situation.

6. Enlarge People

This is another way of saying mentoring. You should look for opportunities to speak into people's lives if you want to be truly influential. Be on the look out for people who:

- Have similar beliefs and aims to you in their life
- You can see potential in
- Are teachable, open and coachable
- Are at the right stage in their career, life or situation to need mentoring.

7. Navigate for People

If you can show people the way forward, you exert a lot of influence. Many people are confused about their direction in work or life. You could possibly suggest what their goal or destination should be. And if they are not sure how to get there, you have an opportunity to help them with that too. If you can ask what someone's dream or vision is, and help them to get there, you have done them a service that will never be forgotten. They won't hesitate to tell others, so boosting your influence and reputation.

"Give, and it will be given to you. A good measure, pressed down, shaken together and running over, will be poured into your lap. For with the measure you use, it will be measured to you."
Jesus Christ, Gospel of Luke, Chapter 6 verse 38
(Holy Bible, New International Version)

8. Connect with People

You connect with others by sharing your experiences and your feelings, and helping them to share theirs. Before you can get people to move on with you, you need to have something in common – some feeling of unity or binding. Look for common ground and common interests to strengthen that connection. Speak from the heart, not just 'management speak' or technical jargon. Say what has been important to you in your development and why. Letting them into your world will deepen your ties. Create a partnership and you will increase your influence.

9. Empower People

Delegating, giving people responsibility, revealing knowledge so the other person can use it too – all these things come under the heading of empowerment. Give people permission to succeed and fail (within sensible limits!). And as they make progress, give them feedback so they can continue learning. If you empower people, you help them grow. If you are growing people, your business should grow – because people are the most important asset of any company. And your influence grows as they spread out into the world and tell others it was you who gave them a chance. There's also another benefit – if others are doing all the jobs for you, that gives you far more choice about what you want to do.

> "As we look ahead into the next century, leaders will be those who empower others."
> **Bill Gates**, US entrepreneur and Microsoft founder

10. Reproduce Other Influencers

The knock-on effect of increasing your influence should be that you create and release other influencers. Many of the world's most successful people can look back to their formative years and identify someone who was a great influence on them.

If you are running a project or company and want to leave a legacy, then you need to be looking to who can take over from you when you move on or retire. Reproducing other influencers in your company gives you a good range of people to select from, and having a range of influencers in your company ensures its future survival.

> "Leadership is based on a spiritual quality; the power to inspire, the power to inspire others to follow."
> **Vince Lombardi**, one of the most successful head coaches in the history of American football (1913-1970)

70 of the Best Tools, Tips and Tactics to Build Your Reputation

Think of some of the world's best known personal brands. Here are the current top 23, in no particular order, in recent surveys:

The Most Famous Icons of All Time, As Voted By Recent Polls

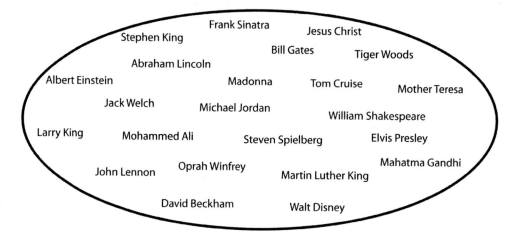

All of these people have developed their reputation in different ways and for different reasons, and have reached iconic status. Some have done it by accident. Some have done it very deliberately. All are famous. And all have built something bigger than themselves. Only one was divine – all the rest were very human! So you can do it too. But given that you're probably not famous yet, you need a few pointers.

You're about to read the very best techniques ever discovered to help you build your reputation. But before jumping in, there are a few final considerations. You see, it would be a big mistake just to pick out the ones you can do, or even the ones you'll enjoy doing. No, you need to be a little more strategic. Choose the right ones for you based on the following five criteria:

1. **Your Reputation Goal.** *Do you want your reputation to deliver you more Pleasure, Profit or Profile?* These techniques will deliver you different results. Make sure you embark on a plan that will deliver you exactly the profile you want!

2. **Your Reputation Strategy.** *How do you want to build your reputation?* You can choose Relationships, Expertise, Propaganda, Understanding, Titles, Actions, Traits, Impressions, Outcomes or Networks. If you are using more than one, what blend of strategies will you use? Which tactics will fit best with your strategies?

3. **Your Position.** *Are you currently employed* (with inherent constraints of time, freedom, expression, compliance, accountability and resources) *or do you have the freedom that comes with self-employed or owner status?* For instance, running a blog is not so straightforward if you have employers. Pick the techniques and tips that fit your personal situation.

4. **Your Personality.** *Some of these tactics will be more up your street, depending on what kind of person you are.* You may be more task-driven than people-driven. You may be very loud and expressive. You may be quiet and unassuming. You may love systems and processes. You may love people

195

and ideas. Utilise those reputation-building methods that make the most of the unique kind of person you are.

5. **Your Strengths.** *What do you find easy that other people find difficult?* What do you really love doing? Do you love writing? Are you a great speaker? Are you strong with details? Are you a voracious learner and reader? Do you hate networking? These skills will dictate which avenues are best for you to build your reputation.

The following tools and tactics are broken down into three 'reputation toolboxes':

Tool Box 1 - Changing Who You Are. *This gives you 11 tips, recommendations and tactics that are either ideals to live up to, wise words for character building or commands to enhance your personality traits.* All will serve to make you more influential and 'reputed'.

Tool Box 2 - Changing What You Do - Anyone. *This gives you 48 tips, recommendations and tactics that apply to anyone looking to build their personal reputation.* Whether you're employed or self-employed, public or private sector, profit or not for profit, product or service driven, the enlightened entrepreneur or the rat-raced corporate executive, you can use many of these tools to enhance your good name and make yourself the 'go to guy' or 'go to girl' for what you do.

Tool Box 3 - Changing What You Do – 'Solopreneurs'. *This gives you 11 extra tips, recommendations and tactics specifically aimed at people with the freedom to really carve out 'go to' status* *in their field.* Typically this would include speakers, coaches, trainers, consultants, trainers, solo-practitioners, writers and entrepreneurs. There are stories, case-studies and quotations to illustrate them. Don't feel overwhelmed by the list. To begin with, select a few of the tips that you can see are easy for you to achieve. Once you begin to crack them, you can move on to others. Reputations are built over time...

Tool Box 1: CHANGING WHO YOU ARE

1. Be Brilliant. This is a fantastic way to build a reputation! Everyone in the above list of icons was brilliant at something. Get really good at something you really love doing, and people will pay you. Remember your reputation is the REP - the Reason Everyone Pays. Whether they pay you Respect, Attention or Money, being brilliant is the start of it all.

 Andy Cope[20], the creator of 'The Art of Brilliance', says: "When I decided what I really wanted to do, I stopped chasing the money. For me, it is about being the best I can and aspiring to be world-class. When I do that, people come back to me time and time again. Why settle for anything less than being yourself, brilliantly?"

2. Develop Persistence. This is bouncing back from adversity. Many a promising reputation has faltered under duress and obstacles. As the old proverb says, smooth seas do not make skilful sailors. There will be failures and setbacks. There will be attacks and insults. There will be times when you don't think your strategies are working. But stick with them. If you've picked the right ones, they will come through for you.

> *"If people knew how hard I had to work to gain my mastery, it wouldn't seem wonderful at all."*
> **Michelangelo**, Renaissance painter and sculptor (1475-1564)

> *"Success is to be measured not so much by the position that one has reached in life... as by the obstacles which he has overcome while trying to succeed."*
> **Booker T Washington**, American political leader, educator and author (1856-1914)

> *"When I hear somebody sigh, 'Life is hard', I am always tempted to ask, 'Compared to what?'"*
> **Sydney J. Harris**, American journalist and author (1917-1986)

3. Know Your Values. Values are what you stand for under pressure. Values are what you believe deeply in. Values are what is right and true for you and reflect what is important in your life. To build the right reputation, you need to make the right decisions. To make the right decisions, you need the right moral compass and the right grounding. You do this through your values, which come from your character.

> *"The world is full of people that have stopped listening to themselves or have listened only to their neighbours to learn what they ought to do, how they ought to behave, and what the values are they should be living for."*
> **Joseph Campbell**, American author, editor, philosopher and teacher (1904-1987)

4. Live and Work Passionately. Passion is contagious. When you love what you do, it makes people want to know you and be around you. When you say you love your work, people take notice. When it's a privilege for you to do your job, you've got something that people may want to part of. There may be millions of other people who do the same type of job as you, but how many are really determined to make a difference in this world through their jobs? If you love to do your job rather than have to do your job, the chances are you already have a great reputation as someone who is good at what they do. That means you will deliver great service and excellent results.

Alison Jones[21] founded The Passion Group to help companies "create inspired people, successful leaders, happy workforces and great company cultures." Her 'I LOVE MONDAYS' fortnightly email brings a ray of sunshine and a burst of inspiration to Monday mornings. When you meet Alison, you see a woman with infectious enthusiasm, who gives everything in life 100%. That's her reputation – she walks it and breathes it. She's a special person to be around. Are you?

5. Aspire to High Standards. Being brilliant is good but it is not enough. There are many brilliant but lazy people. There are many brilliant but poor people. There are many brilliant people who do not achieve their potential. Hold yourself accountable for high standards. Demand more from yourself than other people would demand from you. When your expectations are high, the quality of your work and your interactions will be equally high. As a result, your reputation will soon be exceptional.

> *"There is never much traffic on the extra mile."*
> **Author Unknown**

6. Dream Big Dreams. Entrepreneur Donald Trump says, "If you're going to think, you might as well think big!" Most people can have whatever they want from life. The problem is that when you ask people what they want, they don't know. Most people can tell you what they don't want. Most people have a vague idea that they want to be happier or wealthier but few people reach for the stars. You may never be world-famous. You may never be the 'world's leading...' You may never be the number one. But the higher you reach, the higher you will go! And don't be afraid to dream unrealistic dreams! People who have built great empires often had unreasonable dreams. If you don't aim high, you will never hit a high target. One of the greatest authors of the 17th Century, Thomas Fuller, said that great hopes make great men. Muhammad Ali called it future thinking. Your sphere of influence will increase and your reputation will grow if you aim for greatness and strive for big things.

> *"When you allow yourself to begin to dream big dreams,*
> *creatively abandon the activities that are taking up*
> *too much of your time, and focus your inward*
> *energies on alleviating your main constraints,*
> *you start to feel an incredible sense of*
> *power and confidence."*
> **Brian Tracy**, Canadian self-help author and speaker

"Man, alone, has the power to transform his thoughts into physical reality; man, alone, can dream and make his dreams come true."
Napoleon Hill, one of the earliest authors of the modern genre of personal-success literature (1883-1970)

7. Be Caring. The service you give is related to the person you are. You can 'put on an act' to a certain extent, but when the chips are down who you are will matter more than what you want people to think you are. If you cultivate a caring personality, you will generate a caring business. More than that – you will have an outstanding reputation. If you care as much about your clients' needs as you would about your own – you've cracked it. It's simple but effective. It's called 'the golden rule':

"Do to others as you would have them do to you."
Jesus Christ, Gospel of Luke, Chapter 6, Verse 3
(Holy Bible, New International Version)

8. Ask Yourself the Right Questions. Look at some of the common questions that you ask yourself and turn them into questions that allow you to do something positive. Everyone talks to themselves, and if you're wondering whether you do or not, then you're talking to yourself too! Andy Gilbert splits all self talk into helpful or hindering. High quality questions asked of yourself will either take you close to or further away from your goals. Some typical questions simply need reframing. Entrepreneur Rajesh Setty[22] gives three good examples:

1. Original question: *What am I getting?*
    Reframed question: *What am I becoming?*

2. Original question: *Why is this happening to me?*
    Reframed question: *What can I learn from this?*

3. Original question: *Why can't he/she understand me?*
    Reframed question: *How can I communicate so that he/she can understand me?*

Note also here that the original question is hindering and negative, while the reworded question is helpful and positive. And of course, if you currently don't ask yourself these type of questions at all, you need to. Periodically think through what you are doing and reassess yourself. How are you doing, where are you going and how are you planning to get there?

9. Be Relevant. How many times have your eyes glazed over and your mind wandered as someone has a one-sided conversation with you, telling you nothing you wanted to know? Even if that person started off on a subject that interested you, the waffle you are now hearing might prejudice you against talking to him ever again! *The question is, do you do this to other people?* If you do, you need to stop, unless you want to become known as an utter bore! It could undermine your relationships, your networking and your reputation.

One way of ensuring you are keeping 'on message' for someone is to 'tag your statements'. This simply means not to talk for too long before asking a question. Say something, keep it fairly brief, then bounce it back with a question to check how relevant you are, whether they can identify with the subject and what thoughts they have on the subject. If the response is hardly enthusiastic, you know it's time to change tack.

Relevance is a very important part of your 'likeability factor' and of course you need people to like you if you are going to influence them. Consider relevance in all your contacts with people. Most business people are extremely busy and don't want their time wasted. To know what is likely to be of relevance to someone, you have to get to know them better. That involves caring about them, understanding them and their world, and being prepared to put the time in to find out what is of interest to them. When your focus is more on the other person than on yourself, you will start to understand what is relevant to them.

10. Take Failure in Your Stride. No one can succeed all of the time. Indeed, if you never had failures, the chances are that you wouldn't learn as much. So the important thing is not failure, but your attitude to it and how soon you get over it. Don't allow failure to keep you down – you must get up fast! Often when you look back at failures earlier in your life, they feel far less significant now than they did at the time.

If, at the time of a failure, you can remember that it's more about lessons learned, you're well on the road to recovery. Get it in perspective, and then you can use those lessons to move your reputation forward. Many great reputations have been built on how people overcame failure or disappointment in their lives.

Some of the greatest entrepreneurs have lost millions of pounds and had several projects or businesses fail but they've got back up and made their fortunes all over again. It's your attitude that will make the difference.

> *"Only those who dare to fail greatly can ever achieve greatly."*
> **Robert F. Kennedy,** US Attorney General and Senator
> (1925-1968)

> *"Success consists of going from failure to failure without loss of enthusiasm."*
> **Winston Churchill,** UK Prime Minister and leader during
> World War Two (1874-1965)

11. Be Confident. Every day, thousands of con-artists cheat people out of money and possessions. They cheat their way into positions of influence or jobs they're not qualified for. *Why do people believe them?* Because they sound so convincing. They not only know what to say, they sound as if they believe it. And they sound believable because they believe in themselves. They believe in their own ability to influence and in the power of what they say.

So, if you need confidence to be a confidence trickster, you also need confidence to be an honest influencer. Develop self-belief. Other people won't believe in you unless you believe in yourself. Make sure you know what you are talking about – and then sound as if you know what you are talking about! Don't be arrogant about it, but be assertive.

Tool Box 2: CHANGING WHAT YOU DO - ANYONE

It doesn't matter whether you're employed or self-employed, these 48 tactics, tools and ideas will help anyone build their reputation. Pick a handful and get working on them. If you're already doing them, be more structured and strategic. Choose those that fit together well with your niches and your style. You'll soon be the 'go to' professional for what you do!

1. Write Articles. Magazines, trade journals, local, regional and national newspapers, and association newsletters all need great content to make them interesting. Writing pre-sells others on your abilities, and exposes you to thousands of prospects. And even if you are working for an employer, you can write for these in your own time. If your byline says who you work for, see how much greater respect your company may have for you, as your company bathes in your reflected glory! Also, you may raise your profile in-house by writing for your company's newsletter, in-house literature or intranet.

There are also many internet avenues for writing, such as membership websites, online magazines and papers, professional associations and ezines (electronic magazines or newsletters). They are all crying out for good stories and interesting articles. In the case of the printed page, reprints of published articles make excellent, low-cost sales literature, replacing expensive but less targeted brochures, mailers and newsletters. All of these outlets are looking for content, have column inches to fill and expertise to source. Become a good writer and turn out an article a month to see your expertise elevate!

How do you get started? There are a few different ways. Here's one. Write a 'query letter/email'. This is a letter you write to the editor, outlining the article you wish to contribute and your expertise. Give it an attention-grabbing headline, as editors see bucket-loads of material every day, so it needs to stand out. And make sure you explain how your article will benefit readers. Also ensure your letter says that you will supply the article free (editors have to watch their budgets) on the following conditions:

1. You get a byline (your name is credited as author)
2. Your footnote is included at the end of the article
3. You retain the copyright.

Then ensure that your footnote contains your full contact details and company/personal website address. Retaining copyright allows you to send the same article out to as many other publications as you like. In writing style, try not to sound like you are promoting yourself. If your article reads like one long advert for yourself, you are unlikely to get much take-up from editors. Articles give you far more credibility than adverts. If you succeed at article-writing, it will elevate your reputation far more than paid-for publicity.

Tip. There are two targets for your writing – your current/potential clients and your peers. Think about who you want to be known by most and target that audience. You should be writing differently for recognition amongst your peers than you would for your prospects.

There are also two types of articles. First there are content rich, informative pieces that give plenty of notice that you know what you're talking about. These are chock-full of 'how to' stuff that can make a difference in the readers' business and even personal lives. The inference here is that if you're prepared to give so much for free, there's even more in the bag when they engage you.

Second, there are 'infomercials' or 'advertorials' (advertising editorials). These are essentially sales pieces, thinly disguised as articles. They tell people how good you are and why they should pick up the phone today. You usually have to pay for the space, but not always.

 Rikki Arundel[23] is a founding member and president of the Professional Speaking Association in the UK. She had over 700 articles published throughout the nineties that established her as the technology guru in the financial services industry. She now runs an article directory so she can supply articles to people who want to increase their internet presence and perceived expertise.

Rikki writes, "Article writing is really expanding. I regularly submit articles to about 100 article directories - which helps to drive traffic to my web site and position me as an expert in sales and marketing communications. I run a number of blogs which I write for every week. I also contribute to a number of other sites and post to discussion forums which usually get positioned on Google very quickly. If you search Google for Rikki Arundel, it will produce over 20,000 results. I am not just top position - I take the first 135 places on Google, all of which are unique web sites promoting me, most of them being sites hosting

207

my articles. I do still occasionally write for printed media, but there is so much opportunity now for online writing."
Do you think Rikki's reputation might be pretty powerful?

2. Read Extensively. It has been said that where you end up five years from now will depend on the people you've got around you and the books you've read. *Today's readers are tomorrow's leaders.* You should read everything you can. You can go wide or deep or both. Experts set aside time to read a variety of media that affect their target audience. Consider a speed reading or photo reading course to maximise your precious time. Read trade and special interest magazines and articles - either hard copies or online. They will cover issues affecting your niche and provide focused, up-to-the-minute information.

 Common estimates say the average business professional reads less than a book a year. That's pretty shocking, right? Well, it seems that people are becoming more and more illiterate. Here are some even more shocking statistics on reading from self-publishing guru Dan Poynter[24]. These statistics are for America, which tends to lead the UK and other countries in trends. If these are anything like true for both the UK and the US, then, if you read a lot, you have a massive advantage at your fingertips!

- *A successful fiction book sells 5,000 copies. A successful non-fiction book sells 7,500 copies.*

- *One third of high school graduates never read another book for the rest of their lives. Many do not even graduate from high school.*

- *58% of the US adult population never reads another book after high school*

- *42% of college graduates never read another book*

- *80% of US families did not buy or read a book last year*

- *70% of US adults have not been in a bookstore in the last five years*

- *57% of new books are not read to completion*

- *Only 32% of the U.S. population has ever been in a bookstore*

- *Customers 55 and older account for more than one third of all books bought*

> *"Half of the American people have never read a newspaper.*
> *Half have never voted for President.*
> *One hopes it is the same half."*
> **Gore Vidal**, author

3. Keep Current. Subscribe to e-mail newsletters, blogs, news services and specialised publications. These sources enable you to take the pulse of your industry and keep yourself up-to-date. Developing personally and professionally should be a big part of cultivating and maintaining your reputation.

> *"If the other guys are getting better, then you'd better be getting better faster than the other guys are getting better or by definition, you'll be getting worse."*
> **Tom Peters**, American expert and author on business management practices.

4. Develop a Library. This can be especially effective in any room or place where you meet clients and contacts. Develop a reference collection of quality books. Ones you can turn to for immediate, dependable information. Make frequent trips to a good business bookstore and look for books that address your industry, niche, and type of work. When people see the kind of things you read (even if you have not read every single page of every single book) they will judge you favourably and respect you for your knowledge and commitment to learning.

5. Take Seminars, Courses and Classes. Your continuing education should be life-long to keep you ahead of the chasing pack. Along with some of the top professionals in my key fields (conference speaking and consulting) I invest around 10% of my annual income back into professional development. This helps me stay ahead of the field and work hard to bring new and fresh insight, knowledge and research to my audiences and clients. It's good to stay ahead of the game!

6. Attend Conferences, Trade Shows and Exhibitions. These only take place once a year, and by picking out half a dozen key events over a twelve-month period, you can keep yourself connected to all the people, knowledge and trends you need to be held in high repute. Know who the key players are in your industry and get yourself known by influential people 'in the know'. If you are not self-employed, your company may well be keen to send you to places like this anyway. If they don't, ask them. It's in their interest that you develop professionally.

7. Keep Your Sales Skills Sharp. Your reputation will bring people to you, but you will still have to clinch the deal and close the sale. Everybody is selling something these days, even if you are just selling yourself. Whether you are employed or self-employed, it is difficult to climb into the top 10% of your profession without being able to win more business, create more opportunities or open more doors. You might be a reluctant salesman/saleswoman, but the highest-paid people in professional life tend to be those who sell well.

 Peter has been an independent financial adviser for over 30 years. He knows how loyal other people's clients can be. In the quest for more business, he knows he has to break or undermine existing loyalties. Switch business comes from people who have been with their incumbent adviser for years. He also understands that 90% of the financial products and services he offers are similar to his competitors'. How does he make the difference? He gets good at selling. He says, "Sometimes it's not enough to be good. You need to be able to ask for the business. You need to be confident and courageous enough to invite them to consider the switch. Then you need to be proficient in closing the sale. I've won more business through my selling ability than my product knowledge!"

211

8. Speak Publicly. How good are you at presenting? How comfortable are you performing in front of an audience? There are many organisations and associations that you could offer your services to as an expert. They will run conferences, seminars and workshops. You could also develop your presentations in meetings and pitches. Make your contributions telling, relevant and 'bang in-line' with everything you want people to think about you. If you don't work for yourself, see if there are any speaking opportunities on behalf of your company. If you are really good at it, you may be able to move into a new role.

 Andy Clark[25], founder of the Speakers Academy, confirms that your reputation depends not only on the substance of your message but also on the style with which you deliver it. He says, "Speaking is a skill that everyone has because all that is really needed is the ability to be yourself and relax in front of your audience. Kennedy blew Nixon away because of his ability to present. David Cameron, a relatively untested 'new boy', did the same to David Davies – a clear front runner in the last Tory party leadership contest, whose reputation was of an experienced statesman. If you cannot deliver a powerful message that moves and inspires your audiences, you're not going to be in the game for long."

9. Volunteer for Key Causes and Projects. These could be local community projects or a national or international cause that chimes with your core values. You can do this whether or not you are self-employed, as many voluntary groups meet outside of work time. Your choice of organisation and the role that you take within the organisation will speak volumes about who you are to those around you. Volunteering also raises your profile, because very few people do it. It can open up a whole new area of networking. You may even meet celebrities you wouldn't otherwise be able to contact, because they are often willing to help promote charities.

Ideally, lead a team of volunteers, because it will develop your leadership skills in a way that normal business never can. So consider what cause, person or charity you could possibly devote your time and expertise to.

> *"You really can change the world if you care enough."*
> **Marion Wright Edelman**, the first African American woman admitted to the Mississippi Bar
>
> *"The more you lose yourself in something bigger than yourself, the more energy you will have."*
> **Norman Vincent Peale**, author of 'The Power of Positive Thinking'
>
> *"We make a living by what we get; we make a life by what we give."*
> **Winston Churchill**, UK Prime Minister and leader during World War Two (1874-1965)

10. Sign Up for Business Committees and Assignments. These arise within your workplace or within your industry. They will give you an excellent opportunity to network with new contacts and to showcase your skills and your brand. It will also get your name on research papers, reports, press releases and official documents. If you keep your ear to the ground, you will soon find out what projects need contributors and researchers. You'll also learn which committees need members. A good way to source these opportunities is to talk to people already involved in them. *Fresh blood and support is nearly always welcome!*

 Sam had a mid-level financial role in a large manufacturing company. The board were considering employing an outside consultant to produce a special report on staff appraisal schemes. Sam offered to take up the challenge, which involved forming a small focus group and around 20 extra hours of investigative work and interviews over three months. As a result, her work gained her access to many other people in the company, and raised her profile significantly. Her name was on the finished document, and promotion followed six months later. It also looked strong on her CV.

11. Join Associations, Organisations and Clubs. Joining professional associations gives you a chance to shape policy, get ahead and be a part of new ideas. It allows you to influence and certainly raises your profile. There are literally thousands of these that require a constant flow of new members. They also have great need for a dedicated but select few individuals who will gravitate to the board and invest a little extra time in roles of responsibility. You can also join leisure clubs or special interest groups just in order to get to know the right people. *You appreciate that who you know is more important than what you know.* Joining the golf club where your target clients play may be a business cliché but every cliché arises for a reason.

James had a mid-management role in a large IT company. The prospects for promotion were limited and with a baby girl coming into the family, he knew he had to be a lot more pro-active with his career. He attended a few local meetings of the Chartered Institute of Marketing. Within a short time, he was asked to join the committee and help organise events. He is now Chair of a large region and wields significant influence with a variety of business leaders. From his connections, he has now moved companies and works in an expanded and more challenging role with a much better package.

12. Teach at a Local College or University. This could be Further or Higher Education. There are many part-time and visiting lecturers who have one foot in the world of business and one foot in the world of academia. *It will give you status as an expert and enhance your reputation, as well as gaining you new contacts.* Your current employers, if you have them, might quite like the idea of you raising the profile of the company by dedicating yourself to advancing the local student population. Call your local educational establishments for their prospectuses and identify any programmes and modules you could help with. You might even come up with new ideas and topics you can bring to the table. There may be some 'lead time' between when you first make your approach and when they need you, because staffing is worked out in terms or semesters in advance.

Nadio Granata[26] is Managing Director of a successful networking group, LunchNet, and also a Senior Lecturer in Marketing at a UK university. By blending his business and academic worlds, Nadio has been able to offer his students tremendous opportunities and also make valuable contacts outside the university. He has employed graduates in his business and been able to utilise students in research and development projects that bring businesses into the university, often leading on to things such as student placement, guest lecturers and industry workshops.

13. Stop Saying 'You're Welcome!' If you are good at what you do, you'll know that there have been times when you've really pulled out the stops for a client, customer or contact. Times when you've really gone out of your way. Times when you called in a few favours to sort out a problem for them. When these people tell you you've done a terrific job, as they hopefully will, you'll probably reply with the most common responses – 'you're welcome' or 'it's nothing' or 'all part of the service'. When you do this, it can sometimes devalue your efforts and give an impression that what you did was no big deal. There is a better way. Next time it happens, try a few of these phrases:

- *"That's lovely to hear you say that - we certainly pulled out the stops on this one!"*
- *"What a lovely thing to say! I put a lot of effort into this and I'm really pleased it worked out for you."*
- *"I'm really glad you said that because I worked really*

hard on that project."

- *"It makes me feel great to hear that, because this wasn't an easy thing to do!"*

Make people feel special by telling them it *was* a big deal. If you move heaven and earth for them, and tell them it was nothing, you do your reputation no good at all. Capitalise on these opportunities to let people know you've given great service and really gone out of your way for them. That way, you will go up in their estimation, they will think more of you and be itching to tell others that story!

 Jeff worked in a large law firm in the commercial property department. He came home one day early from his holiday to help finalise an 18-office acquisition for one of his best clients. Instead of keeping quiet about the fact that it was his holiday, Jeff made sure that his client knew. He also made sure that his client was aware that Jeff could have passed this work on to a colleague, but valued the relationship so much that he wanted to handle it personally. Naturally, the client was impressed, and when he thanked Jeff, this was the reply he got: "Hey, I didn't do it for the thanks, but it's great to hear you say it! Truth be known, I didn't have to do this. But I wanted to get this right because I knew it was important for you. I could count on one hand the number of clients I would do this for, and you're one of them."

Think twice before you say 'you're welcome!'

217

14. Gather and Use Testimonials. Generally speaking, you are not the best person to tell others how fantastic you are. Everybody says how fantastic they are and everyone is 'bigging themselves up'. Instead, let others do the talking. It gives you far more credibility. Next time people thank you and say what a good job you've done, recognise that this is a fantastic time to ask for something from them. They may even ask you there and then if there is anything they can do for you. When this happens, here are a few great things to say:

- *"That's lovely to hear you say that. Listen, would you mind putting that in writing?"*
- *"What a lovely thing to say. Would you mind if I repeated that to a few people?"*
- *"I'm really glad you said that because I worked really hard on that project. Would it be okay if I wrote that down and used it for a few business development projects?"*

You should get these endorsements from clients, customers or employers. You could also ask colleagues from other departments, or possibly peers or mentors in your industry. Could you even persuade an outside expert to endorse what you offer? There is nothing that builds credibility so much as a third party recommendation.

 Steve was a relationship manager for the corporate department of a large bank. He was called to attend a particularly important client meeting, but fell ill the day

before. Steve called the client to ask if the meeting could be rearranged, but with the other people present this was impossible. Despite being 'out on his feet', Steve made it for that meeting. Despite feeling like death, he suited up and clocked in. Afterwards, the client said how much he appreciated Steve coming, despite his circumstances. Steve's reply?

"To tell the truth, there were a few places I would rather have been. But I knew I had to be here and I'm really glad I came. And the big thing that swung it for me was that I realised that if ever I needed anything from you, you would do exactly the same for me."

Now guess who is going to find it really easy to get a fantastic testimonial, lots of third party credibility and some great referrals?

> *"Credibility is the believability of a statement, action, or source, and the propensity of the observer to believe that statement."*
> **Anon**

15. Get a Mentor. Not only can a good mentor introduce you to the right people and fast-track your development, but they can show you what roads not to take and which people not to bother trying to influence. A mentor is someone who has been where you are going. A mentor is someone who can speak with a voice of experience. A mentor is someone who has already made the mistakes you will make and learned from them. Who do you know that could speak into your life and would be willing to help you get where you need to be?

Tip. Look out for my new 'Mentoring Bible' which will be out shortly. Keep an eye on the Books & Bibles section of my website: www.thetripsystem.com

16. Understand Marketing. *Marketing is not selling.* It is about raising awareness and putting your message out there. You haven't come this far for you to keep quiet about your personal reputation. You have done a lot of hard work to arrive at a point where you now know exactly who you are, what you are offering, who you are offering it to and why you are unique in your chosen field. If you want to build a strong reputation, you must communicate who you are to your target audience. You must be marketing-minded whenever possible. Jay Abraham[27] is one of the world's leading marketing gurus. Here are a few of his quotes:

"If you're attacking your market from multiple positions and your competition isn't, you have all the advantage and it will show up in your increased success and income."

"Understand that you need to sell you and your ideas in order to advance your career, gain more respect, and increase your success, influence and income."

"The fact is everyone is in sales. Whatever area you work in, you do have clients and you do need to sell."

17. Develop Power Scripts. *A script is a phrase or a question delivered in a certain way at a certain time to bring about a particular response.* Words are incredibly powerful and yours should be in some places attention-grabbing, in others subtle and insightful. Craft and use the great questions and also have strong answers ready for tough questions. Top salespeople and influential leaders use scripts. They say the same things over and over again, whether they realise it or not. Why? Because they know that these words will get results. Scripting also helps you to be 'congruent' and congruency is what helps you to develop a strong reputation.

> *"The worst time to think of the best thing to say is as the words are coming out of your mouth."*
> **Rob Brown**

18. Make Best Use of Business Cards. These are one of the best marketing tools if you use them properly. Whenever you give a business card, ask for a business card. When you are given one, don't just stick it straight in your pocket. Show the person you are interested in them by looking at their card for a few seconds. You might also see something that could be worth asking about. Write relevant information on the card such as when and where you met, and the main point you discussed. These notes will make a big difference when following up with that person, if only to impress them that you remembered who they were. This demonstrates a sincere interest in the other person. Then place it carefully in your pocket or wallet. Don't just throw it in your briefcase or put it in a pocket where it might be forgotten. This lets them know you felt

221

their contact was important. If you make people feel important, you make yourself important to them.

A business card gets seen at least three times - when you hand it over, when they get back from having met you, and when they decide to throw it away or file it. If you network regularly and want to be recognised, think about putting your photo on the card. Research shows that a 'photo card' is less likely to be thrown away. At the very least, your card should utilise both sides - a blank back is a wasted opportunity. Also, make people keep it by including something useful on the card and use it to tell people what you want them to do. You could give them a list of handy tips on your field of expertise with the last one giving them a good reason to contact you for your services. Invite them to look at your web site or get free information. Get them to contact you. Include a list of services, your elevator speech, a free offer, or issue an invite to an event.

On many occasions, your business card is the only tangible reminder of your presence after you have met someone. It's all that's left of you after you've gone. They should know how you help people, the problems you can solve and the key benefits of working with you. Does yours work for you or against you?

Tip. I heard a story about one particularly savvy networker who wrote on the back of his card something like, "Do you remember me? We met at _____. We had a good talk about _____ _____. Give me a call to chat further. I have a couple of ideas that might help you." It's such a simple idea but very effective to make the interaction a little more personal and memorable.

19. Consider Traditional Marketing Methods. Mail shots can be good for you if you know your target audience and where to find them. Postcards can be very effective. There is no nuisance envelope to open and they are instantly readable. You can use them to stay in touch with your customers or contacts by sending greetings, news of events or a marketing message. Sales letters get fewer responses than cards but can still work if you make them of high quality, with a strong headline and an emotional connection to get your audience hooked. Then there's always good old Yellow Pages and advertising. Done in the right way, it can be very effective for raising your profile.

 John Sealey[28], the marketing expert known as 'The Courageous Marketeer', is a very charismatic trainer and speaker on sales and marketing. He is also a man who practises what he preaches. John sends out targeted direct mail pieces and marketing postcards to companies he thinks he can help and add value to. He works hard on the 'copy' for these pieces so that they are engaging, entertaining and readable and encourage the recipients to connect with him. Consequently, when he speaks to his clients about how to win more business through traditional marketing, he can speak with authority and experience. People know what he can do, and they know that what he does works, because he has done it before.

20. Deliver Great Service. This is a fantastic way to build your reputation. Customer or client service is a rather neglected area of business life. The companies and people that get it right can make a huge difference to their repeat and referral business and to the loyalty of their patrons. They create buzz. They generate testimonials. They capitalise on word-of-mouth marketing. You have got to care. You have got to want to make a difference. You've got to look after people. You've got to give them a different and better experience than your competitors. Michael Heppell[29], author of 'Five Star Service, One Star Budget', talks about creating magic moments in everyday situations that get you noticed, remembered and referred. He adds that it does not cost a fortune. Now that sounds like a great way of developing a reputation to me!

 David was an exceptional relationship manager, working with corporate clients in a large bank. One day, a good client phoned him to say that his wife had cancer and a large group of family and friends had decided to do a sponsored bike ride to raise money for Cancer Research. He asked David if he would be willing to sponsor the ride and throw in a few pounds. David said, "No." Then, after a pause, he added, "I'll do the bike ride with you." Can you imagine what that did for this relationship? Can you imagine what this did for David's reputation?

21. Get a Website. Even if you work for someone else, it will showcase all the great things about you that don't fit on your business card. You can update it instantly. No printing or postage costs. It should look professional but it doesn't have to be long - just straightforward information and a message telling your target audience what to do next. Publish your own articles and books on your site, but get people to register with you before allowing them to download free information. You are then building your contact list and your network, which is essential for any serious reputation builder.

You want as many people as possible to find your website, so make sure you register your homepage with a set of keywords that relate to your business. The more key words the better – to increase your hit ratio.

22. Write Your Own Newsletter. This sets you apart and offers valuable information sent by email to your carefully chosen target audience, including the ones who have registered on your web site. This can be sent online as an 'ezine' or offline as a hard copy in the mail. You can offer it free or on subscription at a nominal cost. The idea is to create more interest in you and your services. You can make them personal about you and your take on the world, or topic-oriented, like my TRIP System® ezine on relationship marketing. If you have interesting things to say there is an audience who will read it. It's up to you whether you bring it out weekly, fortnightly, monthly, bi-monthly or quarterly. Frequency is a factor of your commitment to write it, your time to produce it and your content to fill it.

 Here's a tale of three newsletters. First, Clive Gott lives the kind of life that makes really good reading. A motivational speaker, endurance athlete and profound thinker, I have a book of quotes that have just come from Clive. His ezine goes out to thousands of people worldwide, and is one of my favourites for two reasons. One, it is synonymous

225

with the man himself. A wonderful and entertaining man to be around, his ezine allows you to get closer to the man himself. The second reason it's so good is that it's full of thought-provoking and challenging ideas and topics.

Next, media coach Alan Stevens[30] probably has the best PR and media ezine I have ever come across. With a mixture of technology (podcasting) 'how to' content and biting humour, it is probably the only one I drop everything to read when it lands.

Third, Art Sobczak[31] is a wonderfully gifted American who is the world authority for me on doing business by phone. I actually pay for his content, and his hard copy newsletter comes to me every two months. It's priceless!

23. Use Your Email Signatures. Put your tagline, your core message, your UVP on your emails. Your website name and your email address should be consistent. Don't waste the opportunity to send out messages by just signing your name. Add other things to help people remember you.

Tip. You should have a number of email signatures. I have around 20. While you might not need so many, they save time, they personalise your correspondence and they give out the message you want to give out. You can create them easily with your email programme and use them to automate a lot of your systems.

24. Develop Strong Elevator Speeches. *'What do you do?'* This is the most commonly asked question in conversations with strangers the world over. You will be out there with people face-to-face. You need that elevator speech - a short phrase that takes seconds to say but will get you noticed and remembered. It should make your listener want to find out more about you and lead to further conversations and questions. It will be inspired by your personal brand and be natural and delivered in your style. Make it brief, punchy, to the point, and fewer than ten seconds in most situations. Rehearse it in advance and deliver it smoothly and confidently. You have already worked out the benefits to your customers of what you do. Now tell them. Try some of these opening phrases:

- *We help our clients to _____*
- *Our aim is to make/give our clients _____*
- *When our clients/customers need _____ we can help _____*
- *If people are struggling/need help with _____ that's where we step in _____*
- *I show _____ how to _____*

If you can't explain what you do in 17 words or less, then you make it difficult for others to talk about you and utilise you.

25. Be Different With Your Voicemail. If someone has taken the trouble to call, don't just tell them you're out. If it fits with the image you want to create, use the opportunity to tell them about yourself and your service, perhaps even offering a free publication or including a special offer. Make their call worthwhile! At least consider having a professional message, dated and recorded daily. It takes a few seconds and a little discipline, and creates a strong impression.

Tip. Think about what you want your answer phone message to do. Do you simply want it to inform people you're not there? Is it to tell people to call back? Is it to encourage them to leave their name, number and a message so you can call them back? Is it to make them glad they called, even though you're not there? Is it to take the opportunity to educate them a little more on you and what you do that's good, different or better? Whatever it is, you should do it on purpose. The average business professional has to leave and pick up five messages every day. How are you going to stand out?

26. Build Strong Relationships. Everything you need in life, you will have to go through someone else to get it. You have to do it yourself, but you cannot do it alone! You need people and they need you, so invest in relationships to build your reputation. But you must be genuine. People will sense it if you are creating an artificial relationship in order to use them. Trust is the bedrock of relationships – and it takes a long time to build trust, but it can be lost in a moment. Although **Reputation by Relationships** may not be your key strategy, this is not one that you can afford to avoid. Try treating your business relationships like a marriage - you're in this for the long-term commitment! Romance your clients – treat others as you would like to be treated yourself. Get to know what they like, how they like it and the frequency! Value the relationship – be a team. Experience the highs and the lows together. The Bible says, "Rejoice with those who rejoice, mourn with those who mourn" (Romans 12:15). Do the best you can and bring the best out in them.

 International speaker Frank Furness is the most internationally-networked man I know! Frank speaks all over the world on sales and marketing. Before he flies anywhere, he makes contact with his UK clients to check out what subsidiaries and contacts they have in his destination country. He always asks for an introduction and permission to call them. In addition, he connects ahead of time with all of his existing contacts in that particular country to set up meetings and discussions. He wants to go deeper. He wants to know who they know. And he asks! Frank doesn't leave it there. He will be talking to strangers on every mode of transport between his front door and his destination hotel. Frank is great at building relationships. It is because he is a great giver and the great connector that he is able to ask so confidently and so often. You cannot build up something like this overnight. But now is a good time to start.

> *"There are only two types of relationships - long-term and very long-term. The rest are casual transactions. Relationships will sustain only when there is mutual value. One-sided relationships will end sooner or later."*
> **Rajesh Setty**, entrepreneur and author of
> '25 Ways To Distinguish Yourself'

27. Use a Personal Brochure. There are two types of brochure – company and personal. If you're doing a personal brochure, it should be just that - personal. Steer away from too many facts and figures about your product or service. Two thirds of the text should be about your personal story, showing how your experiences have made you a more rounded and capable individual today... someone who your target audience can connect with emotionally. Don't sell on the cover - leave it for the back of the brochure, along with your contact details.

Just a note on the design of brochures and all your materials. Use high contrast, e.g. dark print on light paper, or light print on a dark background. Research shows that this type of layout is more likely to be read than low contrast designs – coloured print on coloured backgrounds or coloured paper. Also, don't use tiny print unless you want to specifically exclude older readers! And it is commonly accepted that frames or borders around text increase the likelihood of being read. Some words are also more effective at grabbing readers. The classic three are 'free', 'save' and 'discover' – use these as much as possible in promotional media.

Tip. A personal brochure is more than a business card and less than a website. It's a one, two or four page document that makes people think they should be doing business with you, or meeting with you or getting to know you. If you do either a company or a personal brochure, remember the golden rule of persuasion. Asserting and claiming is not as powerful as demonstrating and illustrating. So use good stories, case studies, testimonials and examples. Use great benefits. If you just want to list the features of your service, throw it in the bin! A brochure is your portable shop window. What's in yours?

28. Become an Amateur Student of Body Language. Develop a knowledge of gestures and 'tells' which reveal people's thoughts and motives. Maintain good eye contact – it encourages trust! There are many tips and strategies for developing rapport that you could use to build better relationships and make more meaningful connections. All of this is useful in building your reputation. Most people unintentionally undermine their communications with non-verbal cues. But when you know exactly which postures, gestures and movements create trust, respect, and influence, you can avoid such self-sabotage, and instead substitute powerful non-verbal messages. Furthermore, learning to read such cues in others is almost like reading their mind. Learn to do BOTH (control your own body language AND read that of others) and you really have an edge!

> *"I speak two languages, Body and English."*
> **Mae West,** American film star (1892-1980)

29. Become a People Watcher. The general idea is that you look at someone who you have never met before, and you try to guess what their ambitions are, what their quirks are and generally what shapes their life. It means you start taking a keen interest in people. Most of the time you don't even think about it. But if you become more aware of how other conversations in a room are going, you can begin to interpret all kinds of different things. Can you spot who is in charge? Who is bored? Who is interested? Who is buying? Who is selling? Who is connecting and introducing? Who is respected and liked? Who is being intently listened to? Who are the decision-makers and who are the influencers? Developing this awareness will help you do all the right things when you're out there meeting people and building relationships. It will also teach you who has presence and why. Presence helps reputation!

30. Get Around the Right People. Learn how to discern the right associations congruent with the person you want to be known as. Your peers, your colleagues, your friends and your family help to define you. The best reputations in the world can be undermined by ill-chosen connections and poorly-managed relationships.

> *"The key is to keep company only with people who uplift you, whose presence calls forth your best."*
> **Epictetus**, Greek philosopher (55-c.135)

> *"Businesses are made by people. We've proven time and time again that you can have a wonderful shop, and put a bloke in there that's no good, and he'll stuff it up. Put a good bloke in, and it just turns around like that."*
> **Gerry Harvey**, Chairman of the successful Harvey Norman retailing chain of home furniture stores in Australia

31. Take Care of Your Appearance. If you're going to act first class, you have to look first class! Within minutes of meeting you, a new contact will have judged your credibility on what you wear, your haircut, your state of health, your facial expression, your tone of voice and, lastly, your words. Look at the appearance of the people you want to influence and be guided by them. As a general rule, dress 10% better than the people you want to impress.

 Although I knew dress mattered, I didn't really understand the power of appearance until I met Harold Rose[32]. He is a master tailor, a consummate professional and is currently making me my third made-to-measure suit. If you don't think this makes a difference, try it. It's not what the suit makes others think. It's what the suit makes you think about yourself.

32. Ask For Help and Advice. There is a difference between these two terms. When somebody asks you for help, you probably get the feeling that you will have to do something physical. When somebody asks you for advice, you get the impression you will be helping from the neck up. In other words with your brain and not your hands. Both of these are great things to ask for. Few people can build a reputation for anything significant on their own. You cannot afford to wait until people volunteer for your cause. You have to ask. You have to be courageous. You have to be humble. You don't get if you don't ask. And the answer to every question you don't ask is 'no!'

"Most people don't ask for help and beat themselves to death trying to figure out everything alone. This is not required. There are so many people out there who have the right knowledge and resources to solve your problems or open new opportunities for you. When you ask for help, it gives you humility. You just need to be ready to give when it is your turn."
Rajesh Setty, entrepreneur and author of
'25 Ways To Distinguish Yourself'

33. Write a Blog. This is becoming a very hip and trendy thing to do, both for employed and self-employed professionals. A blog is a web log, or online journal. It gives you a voice and raises your profile. You can share your thoughts, comment on anything and shape thinking. My blog is on relationship marketing and the TRIP System®. Some blogs command influential, worldwide audiences of thousands. Professional and amateur journalists even use blogs to publish breaking news. It is fairly easy to set up, and if you would like to be more prolific and ubiquitous, this is an excellent and very modern way to do it.

Leading blogging website www.blogger.com *says this: "A blog is a personal diary. A daily pulpit. A collaborative space. A political soapbox. A breaking news outlet. A collection of links. Your own private thoughts. Memos to the world. Your blog is whatever you want it to be. There are millions of them, in all shapes and sizes, and there are no real rules. Since blogs were launched almost five years ago, they have reshaped the web, impacted politics, shaken up journalism, and enabled millions of people to have a voice and connect with others. And we are pretty sure the whole deal is just getting started."*

Graham Jones[33] is an experienced author, speaker and consultant on the Internet. He's written eleven books about the Internet and speaks widely on Internet marketing and Internet psychology. He's a lecturer in psychology and has studied how people interact online. He is utterly convinced of the power of blogs for almost everyone in every situation! "I have several web sites and ten different personal blogs as well as several 'super blogs'," he says.

"As well as raising my profile and reputation with the right people, several actually help generate a spare time income."

34. Be Prolific. This describes someone who is fruitful and highly productive – someone who generates ideas or works frequently and in large quantities. People who do a lot of things generally build a good reputation. This takes a certain amount of discipline and application. You will not develop a great reputation sat on your butt watching television. It is said that there are three kinds of people: those that watch things happen, those that make things happen and those who simply say, "What happened?" Get things done, make things happen and be productive if you want to develop a strong reputation.

35. Develop Your Skills. In his book, 'The Seven Habits of Highly Effective People', Dr Steven Covey calls this *sharpening your saw*. In this fast-moving world, skills can become obsolete quite quickly. The computer skills you had three years ago are largely redundant with the modern software packages and applications. The marketing skills and methods you utilised not so long ago are now less effective with a more sophisticated and discerning marketplace. You need to upskill and stay ahead of the game. Learning languages, mastering modern technology, touch typing, writing, presenting, networking and time management are all key areas you must develop to stay current. Without these, your ability to develop the reputation you want may be severely hindered.

"Today, many companies are reporting that their number one constraint on growth is the inability to hire workers with the necessary skills."
Bill Clinton, former US President

235

36. Become an Expert at Something. The more you become known as a source of expert information, the more potential clients and customers will trust you. You become part of their world, a centre of influence, and because people like to do business with people they know, or know of, you will be their first choice. What could you become the best at? What could you become famous for? What do you find easy that other people find difficult?

Charles Steinmetz was once called out of retirement by General Electric to help them locate a problem in an intricate system of complex machines. Having spent some time tinkering with them and testing various parts of the system, he finally placed a chalk-marked 'X' on a small component in one machine. G.E.'s engineers promptly examined the component, and were amazed to find the defect in the precise location of Steinmetz's mark. Some time later, G.E. received an invoice from the wily engineer – for $10,000. Incredulous, they protested the bill and challenged him to itemise it. Steinmetz did so: "Making one chalk mark: $1," he wrote. "Knowing where to place it: $9,999."

37. Cultivate a UVP (Unique Value Proposition). Your Elevator Speech and your Unique Selling Proposition lay the groundwork for your UVP. They say what you do and how you do it, but your UVP brings in the extra dimension of values over benefits. It goes deeper and it positions you in the marketplace. You need to ask great questions of the people you want to influence to see what value you bring to their life. Online encyclopaedia Wikipedia states that "a value proposition in business and marketing is a statement summarising the customer segment, competitor targets and the core differentiation of one's product from the offerings of competitors." Your UVP says what you do differently and why people should care. Unless you get that straight in your own head, your reputation will be dissipated and fragmented. Your UVP is different from your mission. The mission should define why you exist, but the UVP defines why the right people should care that you exist.

> *"Positioning is the single largest influence on the buying decision."*
> **Geoffrey Moore**, Silicon Valley-based technology consultant and author

38. Coach, Help and Mentor Others. There are three great reasons why this works in building up your reputation. First, when you teach others, it makes you better and drives your skills and knowledge deeper into yourself. You always have to stay at least one step ahead of your pupils! Second, it means you're giving back, and when you're giving, you're living. Third, this gives you your biggest chance to be persuasive and influential, and that makes for a great reputation. Some people doubt this approach because they believe that if you share everything (including your sources of information or help), people won't need you anymore. Won't helping others make you dispensable, and speed others on their way to overtaking you? The answer is that, if you don't help when asked, people will find someone else to help them. Or, with all the information resources available today, they'll find the same information by a different route. It's then you who loses out on the chance to earn a reputation for helpfulness and knowledge,

237

and to spread your influence. And you will have the satisfaction of having helped someone else to grow.

39. Become Great With Your Time. Stress is the feeling of being overwhelmed, with far too much to do and having too little time to do it in. In fact, 'time poverty' is the biggest single problem facing most professionals today. You simply do not have enough time to fulfil all your responsibilities. Because of budget limitations, staff cutbacks, downsizing and competitive pressures, you are forced to take on more and more work, all of which appears to be indispensable to the smooth functioning of your company and department. The solution to this problem of work overload is for you to become an expert on time management. There is probably no other skill that you can learn that will give you a 'bigger bang for your buck' than to become extremely knowledgeable and experienced in managing your time. If you want to build a strong reputation, you'll need to give it the time and energy it deserves. If you're going to waste it, you might get there, but it's going to take you a lot longer!

> *"It has been my observation that most people get ahead during the time that others waste time."*
> **Henry Ford,** pioneer US vehicle manufacturer (1863-1947)

> *"You can do so much in ten minutes' time. Ten minutes, once gone, are gone for good. Divide your life into ten-minute units and sacrifice as few of them as possible in meaningless activity."*
> **Ingvar Kamprad,** founder of IKEA

"Time is our most precious asset, we should invest it wisely."
Michael Levy, US-based English inspirational author

"Perhaps the very best question that you can memorize and repeat, over and over, is, 'What is the most valuable use of my time right now?'"
Brian Tracy, Canadian self-help author and speaker

40. Use Lead Generation Marketing. Reputation is all about selling yourself. But traditional blanket advertising, although it has its place, is usually not the most cost-effective form of marketing. You might spend a huge amount of money and get a lot of phonecalls, perhaps even some sales – but how much long-term business? What you need is to find out what makes the right clients come to you with the minimum possible expenditure, in time or money, on your part. 'Lead generation marketing' is one way of doing this. It usually involves offering something free that will only be of interest to the type of client you want to attract. It could be a free report, a free tip, a free product or service – but it is designed to attract people within your niche. So you generate leads, and it is then up to you to turn these contacts into clients.

In the age of the Internet, this approach has more potential than ever before. For example, my niche is relationship marketing. If I have a 'Free Report on Relationship Marketing' on my website, anyone doing an Internet search for Relationship Marketing material is going to find my site. If they fill in their contact details in order to get their report, I have a new prospect. And it didn't cost me a thing. They spent their time to find me.

If you are going to spend money on advertising, use lead generation adverts. Instead of a large, glossy, expensive main-page advert, try a small, inexpensive classified ad in the section appealing to your target market. Your message needs to be concise, offer an immediate benefit (usually something free) and how to get it. Think: what can you offer your potential clients that will grab their interest? In this information age, it is better to offer useful information rather than a product. Remember: the cost of giving away free reports or tips is far less than the cost of mass marketing, and it generates better leads. You also boost your reputation if people see you are willing to give something away that will help them in their work or life.

41. Advertise in Niche Publications. Whatever type of advert you are considering, whether it's traditional or lead-generating, don't use the general press. Find out what the specialised publications are in your field. A general newspaper or magazine will be read by too many people not in your target market. They are also only skimmed by the reader, looking quickly for things that take their interest, whereas a specialist publication will be read more carefully. Someone who has bought a special interest publication will read it from cover to cover, especially if the subject matter will help them in their work. They want to 'get their money's worth', as specialist periodicals often cost more than high-circulation general publications. Don't just look on the high street shelves – check out the library or the Internet for more occupation-specific or industry-specific publications.

42. Extend Your Network. We have already looked at various aspects of networking, but it's a huge subject and I don't intend to cover it in full in this book – see my website www.thetripsystem. com for information on many relevant resources. But I do want to cover strategic alliances here – as this is a great way of extending your influence and building your reputation.

It's great to extend your own contacts list in as many ways as you can, but you only want to reach people who will be interested in using your services – otherwise you can waste a lot of time and money on printing, packing and postage, or phoning or sending out emails. You can buy in mailing lists that cover the demographic you are targeting, but not the 'psychographic'. For example, your target demographic might be bankers – but your psychographic is the section of those bankers who are likely to want your service or product (due to their interests, attitudes and opinions). This proportion of a demographic could be quite small. This is where forging partnerships or alliances comes in (a pay-off from all that networking!). It's a more cost-effective way of extending your reach. Find other companies that you can work with, that share the same market without directly competing with you.

You need to be careful about data protection legislation, but it may be possible to trade lists of clients or prospects with other companies who work in your field. These will have to be 'opt-in' lists – where clients have given permission for their details to be shared. Alternatively, you could agree to exchange endorsements or special offers – 'you scratch my back and I'll scratch yours'. Adverts could be placed on each others' emails, websites, ezines or letters. In this way you both reach each others' clients or customers legally, because you are not being given their details until they contact you. Other ways include exchanges of posters, flyers, coupons and other printed materials for distribution at each others' offices, exhibitions and events.

Another form of alliance might be with educational institutions. It's better to 'get them while they are young' rather than try to 'teach an old dog new tricks'. In other words, if you can get known by students before they qualify, you can become their first reference point when they start work. In this way you get the first bite at the cherry, before your competitors. For example, if your clients are accountants, ask the institutions who train accountants if there is anything useful you can add to the courses. You could offer a free talk and hopefully get it integrated into the course in future years. In return, you could leave students with your contact details for the future, but more importantly you have made an impression.

43. Underpromise and Overdeliver. Setting the right expectations is a pre-requisite for success. If you set unrealistic expectations, even the greatest plans can fail. Every project is dependent on one or more other projects or people; a delay in one project or by one person can cause a domino effect on all other aspects of your project. The better you can be at estimating the possible points of breakdown in a project, the more you will be able to give realistic promises – and so deliver on them. Failure to hit a client's deadline or falling short in other expectations of a client can have catastrophic effects on your reputation. To grow a reputation – build fail-safes and back-ups into your project plans so that you never fall below expectations, and aim to exceed your client's expectations every time.

44. Focus on Outcomes. Sometimes you can get so bogged down in activities that you look back at the end of the week and don't see any achievements. Planning your week for outcomes is the way to overcome that. In whatever sphere of work, we are rewarded for outcomes, not for activities. So check if all your activities are leading to outcomes. And ask yourself, "What do I want to achieve this week?" Adjust what you do each week if you don't see enough outcomes.

45. Think Long-Term. You can distinguish yourself from the rest by refusing to adopt short-termism. If you don't already plan your year out, rather than just your week, now is the time to start! Also, think of your life-long goals. When someone asks you what you do, wouldn't it be more interesting to answer in those terms than in just what type of work you are involved in? It says a lot more about who you are and is likely to make a much greater impression on someone. If you've never set out your goals in life, again, it's time to start now! And make sure you work out a plan of how to achieve those goals – otherwise dreams never turn into reality. If you have difficulty in this area, you could speak to a life coach. Life coaching is a growing trend so you shouldn't have any difficulty finding a coach.

46. Think Big Picture. Whether you work for a company or run your own, seeing how your work fits in the overall industry picture is illuminating. Keeping in touch with what is happening in your industry – what the trends are – will help you stay ahead of the game. If your type of work is beginning to be done differently, or something new has come along which may outmode the work you do – you may need to rethink what you do. The answer might be retraining to keep up-to-date and ahead of the field, or buying in new equipment or machines, or even jumping ship and changing career entirely. But if you don't know what's going on across your industry outside of your niche, you'll probably miss the boat.

47. Improve as Well as Innovate. Entrepreneurs love to make big changes, make their mark and then move on to the next big thing. But too much change, too fast, can be just as damaging to a company as too little change, too slowly. Innovation is not over once the project has been launched – perfection is never achieved overnight. A great innovation can be undermined by poor implementation. Continuous improvement ought to be a standard part of your vocabulary. The key is to balance innovation with continuous improvement. Take a look at your company or the company you work for as a whole and see if there is enough innovation, and is each innovation being continually reviewed and improved? Note you should also have a tolerance for failure. Innovation is a risky business. If you don't allow for a failure rate, you aren't going to encourage anyone to take risks. And if you're your own boss – emotionally detach yourself from your failures – so you can move on to the next innovation.

48. Influence the Influencers. Whenever you are presenting an argument, an idea or a proposal – it is natural to direct it towards the decision maker. Obviously it is he or she that you are trying to persuade, as they 'hold the keys'. But don't forget the influencers in a group. Sometimes they are the real key holders. Their opinion might have a strong hold over the decision maker. In any group, there will always be one or two people who are the most influential. Typically, the group will look to these people for guidance before forming their own opinions on a subject.

So how do you know who the influencers are? Body language is one way. Next time you are talking to a group and you introduce some issue that requires a stance one way or the other, look around. Most of the group will be looking for non-verbal cues from the influencer. This might be a nod or a shake of the head while you are speaking. If the group see the influencer is nodding, most members of the group are likely to agree with what was being said at that point. If he is shaking his head, most will disagree, like him, with the point made. This scenario will help you see who you should be trying to persuade! The cues may be much more subtle, or, sometimes, much more verbal! But if you can influence the influencers, you are engaging them in spreading your influence.

Tool Box 3: CHANGING WHAT YOU DO – 'SOLOPRENEURS'

These tools are almost exclusively for people in business for themselves, or at least at the head of their company. They have huge autonomy and influence over their reputation as it comes 'top down'. Sometimes these tools can be utilised by employed professionals, but there's just a little more politics involved!

1. Give a Guarantee. This is not always possible, but if you are confident in what you provide, some kind of risk reversal can provide instant credibility for you and assurance for your prospective client who feels in control of the business relationship.

 Chris Cardell[34] is one of the UK's leading experts on business growth and marketing. He has recently launched a membership website with this guarantee: "So here's my promise to you. Go to my Private Members Client site. When you get there, join up. It's so cheap; it's ridiculous at £29.95 plus VAT per month. You can cancel anytime – but that's not all. Once you join, if you're not convinced that the material will make you at least ONE THOUSAND POUNDS (trust me, it will make you much more) we will refund your payment in full, no questions asked. In other words, I'm guaranteeing you a return on your investment of more than 3,000%. But please don't take my word for it. Put me to the test and let's create the business success that you deserve. If you can't immediately see how the material you are about to access will make you one thousand pounds (remember, I'm aiming for tens or hundreds of thousands) I will refund your payment in full, no questions asked."

2. Articulate a Distinct Viewpoint. It's not enough just to be an expert. You need to use your knowledge to deliberately distinguish yourself from your competitors. Plug yourself into every possible outlet that influences your niche. Assess what others are doing, saying, and writing about your industry. Your goal is not just to be fully informed, but also to develop a keen perspective that sees links between your industry and the larger world. Experts know that they must actively seek out new evidence that impacts on their theories and assumptions. You don't need an ultimate truth, but you do need to articulate your position clearly and have relevant facts close at hand. An expert always champions a particular point of view. It's not just about knowledge – it's the application of that knowledge that takes you places with your personal brand.

 Michael was a marketing professional who was trying to gain more PR through local and regional papers and magazines. Unfortunately, his article ideas and pitches fell on deaf ears. He gave great solutions to problems the readers posed, but he never got a call to pursue things further. Then he started being more controversial with his advice, and within hours was being called for his views as an expert.

> *"5% of people probably won't like you no matter what you do. 5% will love you no matter what you do. What can you do to engage the vast majority? You have to be a little different!"*
> **Nigel Risner**[35], British motivational speaker

3. Hire a Publicist. A PR consultant or agent will help you regularly comment on important issues in your field. Publicity is better than advertising, principally because it implies objective approval. You are not selling your product or service. You are being sold as an expert by a third party. Great publicists can be worth their weight in gold.

Tip. I decided I wanted to raise my profile in my local area. In three months, my publicist, Kate Broad[35], secured me four radio interviews, an appearance on national television, several articles in local and regional publications and a one-to-one lunch with the editor of a prestigious business magazine. Think what that might do for your reputation!

4. Make Appearances on Radio and Television. There are now so many channels that producers don't have enough guests to fill their air time. TV and radio work is not as difficult to do as you might think. Many local and national stations are looking for experts in all kinds of areas. They need credible comments and analysis on the many different events that take place every day. Why shouldn't that expert be you? If you now occupy a narrow niche, researchers will search you out for their programmes. Programme producers love contributions from people who are uniquely qualified in their speciality. If you aren't getting any invitations onto radio or TV, try offering your services to them.

A hair transplant doctor sent out a press release to all the TV stations, offering to perform surgery live on air. A medical documentary series accepted his offer, and with the patient's permission, the surgery was filmed and broadcasted. The surgeon was flooded with calls afterwards. He also asked for a copy of the programme, and permission to produce copies to send out to potential customers. Nowadays, it would also be a good idea to get

the footage on his website so people can view it online, saving him copying and postage costs.

Top media coach Alan Stevens says, "People don't realise how easy it is to get on the TV or radio. Here's what to do in three steps. First, listen to the output and look for regular slots which fit your expertise. Second, find a connection between what they are broadcasting and what you do. This is called doing your homework. Third, contact the station editor and volunteer your services and your story to the appropriate programme."

5. Produce Quality Materials. Everything you produce says something about you. The cliché that you never get a second chance to create a good first impression fully applies to all of your business marketing efforts. So go for quality with your business cards, mail-outs, letters, adverts, websites and e-mails. Produce them all professionally. Do you want to be thought of as cheap? NO. Then don't put out cheap branding material.

Tip. When you provide a service such as consulting, banking, legal or financial advice, you have no showroom, no shop window, no tangible products and nothing to touch or feel. So you must communicate in different ways what you do, what you know and how you can help. Your materials, your website, your emails and your correspondence all say something about you. They are your shop window, and you have to make them count.

6. Be Consistent. Make sure you are consistent across your logos, your letters, your emails, your marketing literature, your business

249

cards and your website. Give a clear and consistent message to your target audience. What will someone think if they are all totally different? Perhaps your business is equally haphazard? Articulate your core message and market that consistently across all media. In general, people like to know what they are getting. Trust comes from familiarity rather than surprises. Keep everything together and you will find your reputation becomes more and more what you want it to be.

> *"Trust men and they will be true to you; treat them greatly and they will show themselves great."*
> **Ralph Waldo Emerson**, American author, poet, and philosopher (1803-1882)

7. Consider Yellow Pages. Once your reputation is hitting the roof, don't think you've left behind the little ways of being 'out there'. What's the use of people knowing who you are and how great you would be for them, if they can't remember your name, have mislaid your web address or can't find you on Google? In these days of the internet, it may seem less important to be in the Yellow Pages, your Thomson Local or even the phonebook (which these days is organised much better to find businesses). But whether it's these or trade directories, local business directories or trade publications, make sure your company is listed in as many of them as possible. If paying to be in a directory, you don't need a special, big advert. The important thing is to be in there. But do get listed under as many different categories as you think people might look under for your service. The same applies to advertising on the web. You should get on as many different search engines as possible.

8. Get a Great Name. If you want 'front-of-mind' awareness to distinguish you from the rest, then the name of your product or service must come to mind instantaneously. How memorable is yours? My top tip here is: learn from the experience of others. If you study the top 100 brands in the world at any given time, then the chances are that only one or two of these say exactly what they do. In other words, about 98% of the top brands' names do not reveal the nature of the products or services they offer. What this means is this: they can stand out amongst their competitors and their brands are more likely to be memorable. Your first reaction might be, "I'm not a global business, I've not got a huge budget and I need to let people know what I do". As a result, you might want to choose a name that is simple and describes what you do. Hang on a minute, though! Actually, this is what most businesses do: have a look in a directory, like Yellow Pages, in any classification and see how many businesses have names that describe what they do.

If this is what most businesses do, why merge into a sea of blandness? Why not be different and make your name stand out? As a consumer, what businesses do you remember most? My guess is that, taking banks and loan companies as an example, you will remember Egg, Cahoot and Smile much more than the 'loans company' style business names. So, getting a strong and different branding for your business is going to help in the long run because your customers are going to remember your name better and you will stand out from your competitors. Not only that, but from a legal point of view your ability to protect and enforce that brand will be so much stronger.

251

For help on creating and protecting brands, have a look at the IMPACT® blog of UK law firm Freeth Cartwright LLP. It is at http://impact.freethcartwright.com and the branding category is the place to look.

9. Create a New Category. Have you built your marketing strategy around your particular brand within a well-known product or service strategy? The only problem with that is you get drowned in a sea of competitors. How are you going to stand out? Rising to the top among all those others is going to be hard work. But if you create your own category, you can be the expert in that field, because you have become unique. You have differentiated. If you can be the first to cater to a new market, or the first to create an alternative service, then you are suddenly in a category with no competitors! This might not be as difficult as it sounds. It may only be a case of adjusting or customising your existing product or service, rather than doing something entirely new. But the important thing is that it is perceived to be new or unique or the first. And perception is more important than reality. The best products or services don't always win – only those that are perceived to be the best.

> *"Marketing is not a battle of products but a battle of perceptions."*
> **Jack Trout and Al Ries**, co-authors of the pioneering book on positioning: 'Positioning: The Battle for Your Mind'

For example, looking at your clientele can be one way of deciding on your unique category. If you are a financial advisor and you see that your most profitable business, or the majority of your business, is with a particular type of client – why not market yourself exclusively to that sector? E.g. 'Joe Bloggs – the leader in financial services to dentists', or 'the dentists' choice for finance', or 'creator of the first comprehensive dental financing package'. Check there are no other financial advisors saying the same thing, and you have done it! You will attract more and more dentists, because you will be perceived as the 'go to' service for dentists. In short, how you package yourself is crucial. It is how today's brand names have gone from obscurity to being perceived as the best.

10. Turn the Ordinary into Something Extraordinary. In today's saturated market, telling someone that you are the best or unique doesn't carry much weight – everyone's saying it. In fact, it may even count against you, because saying so directly can make you appear potentially dishonest or prone to exaggerating. But give a unique name to your product or service, and perhaps trademark it, and you will cast your service in a unique light to all the rest. It will not only be intriguing, but perceived as something new – something perhaps that your potential client is missing out on. In other words, you create a demand. And you create an impression that you are an expert in your field, because you have something that no one else has. Taking it even further, you could even register your trademark so that you legally protect it from copycats.

Another way of turning the ordinary into the extraordinary is to highlight. Think of some aspect of your service that is always given as a matter of course, but is never highlighted. Your competitors may give exactly the same service, but do they say so? If not, then you can! Prospects may guess that this aspect of service comes as par for the course in your industry, without any extra payment, but may not be sure. If you highlight the fact that you do it and do it for free, you reassure your prospects. And as you are the only one giving that reassurance, they are more likely to choose you.

Additionally, consider naming this part of your service to make it sound special. For example, most opticians offer free eye tests when buying spectacles. Most people know that, but may not be aware the test includes a test for glaucoma for those over 40. But if an optician calls this 'Free Comprehensive Eye MOT and Glaucoma Test' – or something similar – it will be perceived as superior. It also informs the potential customer of an added benefit they may not have been aware of.

11. Expand Within Your Niche. Once you have determined your niche and you are exploiting it, it may be time to consider expanding the range of options you give your clients. This doesn't mean adding new things outside your niche – that would defeat the whole point of niching. It means looking at the services you provide within that niche and seeing if they can be broken down further. In other words, you may currently specialise in service A-Z, but there may be some clients out there who just want to buy A-F, G-M or N-Z – or even just Z! If smaller parts of your service can be offered in a cost-effective way, you can expand your market while remaining in your niche.

That's 70 fantastic and powerful ways to build and maximise your reputation. Now, assuming your reputation is on track, it's where you want it and things are going well, let's look at what might go wrong and how you can defend and evolve your reputation.

Section 4: DEFENDING REPUTATIONS

What Damages Your Reputation

Your already know that your reputation is one of your most valuable assets. So how come so many reputations get damaged, battered and faded? Let's investigate.

Your reputation is what people judge you by. It helps them decide whether they will use you, buy you, associate with you and recommend you. Just because you have a good reputation, it doesn't mean it will always be that way. There are two enemies who can destroy or damage your reputation. The first is you. The second is others.

It can be done with malice, planning and deliberation (jealousy, revenge, hatred, protection) in an act or acts of sabotage. It can be done needlessly, ignorantly, carelessly and complacently, over time or in a one-off hit.

Read this paragraph carefully! There will be people who attack not just you but everything you stand for. It's up to you to defend against this IF YOUR REPUTATION IS IMPORTANT! They attack you sometimes *not because they hate you, but because they're not you and they want to be.* Or perhaps because you being you is stopping them from being them. Or it could be because you being you is stopping them from being who they want to be - if you follow me!

Here are the top ten ways you could damage your own good name and set your reputation back several years!

1. Over-Committing and Letting People Down

You can't be all things to all people. Take a step back and refocus, or burn out! Learn to say no and be as assertive as you need to be. Think carefully about what you say yes to, because some things will naturally help your reputation, some will be neutral and some will hinder. Choose wisely.

2. Bragging, Asserting and Claiming Instead of Demonstrating and Illustrating

If you keep saying you're great, you have to back it up or back off. People want proof. That's why Muhammad Ali was the best – he named it and claimed it! And of course, 'it ain't bragging if you've done it', but people still resent any over-enthusiastic self-appreciation.

256

3. Failing to Follow Up as Promised

This is an erosion of previously high standards – things begin to slip. Be careful what you promise and beware of multiple deadlines. They will catch up with you! It's a much-used phrase, but under-promising and over-delivering is a fabulous way to operate! Follow up correspondence, make follow-up calls and connect with referrals as quickly as you can. Speed stuns!

4. Not Doing What You Say You'll Do

This is a measure of integrity – doing what you say you'll do, whether you like it or not. A more hard hitting definition of integrity is doing what you say you're going to do, long after the emotions which accompanied your pledge have subsided. Too often you promise service levels, deeds and deadlines in times of confidence, positivity and even euphoria! Like saying you're going to run a marathon, you get all fired up with images of finishing lines and success. When the good feelings and positive vibes quieten down, it's down to you, your running shoes and the road!

5. Displaying Arrogance

If you think people will always revere you, you're wrong. People can be fickle and easily swayed in this age of low trust and low loyalty. You can go out of fashion very quickly if you're not careful. There are too many reputation gravestones of professionals and celebrities who thought they would live forever! One mistake, whether it be of their own making or of others, can bring them down. Stay humble and remember where you came from.

6. Becoming Complacent

Remember the way you used to handle referrals, compliments, PR and the 'little people'? Have you become too big for your boots? Have you become condescending and patronising? Have you forgotten where you came from? Have you forgotten your allies? Have you burned bridges? Set the record straight, reach out and reconnect.

7. Becoming Bored and Unchallenged

You could become something you really wanted to be, only then to lose the edge to continue. You could achieve what you wanted only to find it's the journey more than the destination. I love the quote from actress Lily Tomlin: 'You might win the rat race, but you're still a rat!' Keep fresh and challenged, and stay ahead of the game if you want to keep leveraging your reputation. Do you want people to say about you, "He's great, but you should have seen him five years ago" or would you rather they said, "I saw him five years ago and he's a hundred times better now"?

8. Becoming Careless

Be careful what you say, do and write. Your thoughts can so easily end up in the public domain. Ask any politician how many times they've said or written something which came back to haunt them. From diaries to blogs to books, to online forums, to articles, to on the record and off the record interviews, to formal and informal conversations, everything can appear in the public domain. And all can trip you up if you are not careful.

9. Exercising Clouded Judgement

The more famous or 'reputed' you become, the higher up you go. The higher up you go, the further you may have to fall. And as you become a more attractive proposition, all kinds of opportunities, offers, projects and enticing proposals will come your way. Some will be good. Some will be bad. Some will be good for your name. Some will be bad for your name. You may choose the wrong one. You won't be the first or the last! Pray for wisdom!

10. Picking the Wrong Fights

Is it possible you could climb to the top of the ladder, only to find it's leaning against the wrong wall? Ever chased rainbows and missed the pot of gold? The biggest mistake is to go after the wrong reputation. You may well become somebody you never intended to be. When I do consultations with my clients on their reputation campaigns, I often find they're after becoming something that is really not their destiny! Get in a war you want to win. And fight the battles you want to fight. Then you can be sure you'll have the reputation you truly desire.

Even before your reputation comes under attack, you should prepare with a strong, proactive defence. Build good walls and it will make people think twice about attacking, and make attacks less successful. You'll hopefully be more diligent and mindful of what you yourself can do to undermine your good name! Let's see in more detail what you can do to defend your reputation.

How to Defend Your Reputation

When it comes to other people trying to bring down your good name, a great PR consultant goes a long way. People can be jealous, competitive, angry, misguided and vicious if they feel threatened or aggrieved. In some circumstances, they may even be justified. The point is that attacks will come. They will either be subtle and carefully orchestrated, or brutal and unpremeditated.

There are two strategies for defending your reputation. One is proactive, and the other is reactive.

Proactive Reputation Defence

This is used when you prepare in advance for deliberate or accidental damage to your good name. You have to do everything in your power to minimise the impact, possibility and brutality of the damage.

Reactive Reputation Defence

This is used when you've suffered damage and you need to put it right after the event. This is crisis management for which there are experts. I'll give you a few ideas!

Of course, the proactive approach will create the least impact and be the least costly! To utilise this plan, you need to prepare yourself with scripts, exit strategies, coping strategies and allies. While a full assault on all of these is beyond the remit of this book, you might want to consider your answers to the following *eleven best questions for Proactive Reputation Defence:*

1. Who might want to damage your good name and why?
2. How vulnerable does the Internet make you?
3. What allies, spies and moles do you have who can tell you what people are really saying about you?
4. What enemies, spies and moles might be in your inner circle that could undermine your best reputational efforts?
5. What research can you do to see what people are really saying about you online?
6. When are the best times to react and the best times to stay silent?
7. What is your relationship with the media and how could you improve it?
8. What professionals (PR consultants, technology experts, legal experts) could you build a relationship with now in case you need them in the future? (If you need a great one, ask me!)
9. How can you improve your own persuasion and presenting skills so you can speak with authority in public if and when you need to?
10. What can you do in advance of a crisis or attack?
11. How can you communicate with your customers and clients if you need to set any record straight?

If you can answer these now, you might see things coming. If you do not have answers to these questions, you may be putting your reputation at unnecessary risk. Alternatively, you may be supremely confident that none of the above applies to your situation. As long as you can protect what you work hard to build and you know how to handle a crisis, your reputation should remain strong and powerful. That means it will serve you many a long year and beyond!

What can you be doing to ensure these questions have minor or no implications for your reputation strategy? *A little proactivity goes a long way with your reputation.* If you look after it well, you probably won't need to deal with a crisis! Good reputation management will keep you ahead of your competitors and maintain your position as the obvious expert in your field. *Here are the 10 best ways to keep yourself ahead of the game:*

1. Keep on Top of Your Reputation. *Constantly seek feedback and opinion* from people you admire and trust, and from people who count. Look at your marketing materials regularly. Update all of your photographs every couple of years. Put the vanity to one side and ensure that you look like 'you'. You want to be recognised, don't you?

2. Innovate. *Stay fresh and stay challenged.* Get involved in new projects. Complacency can be a killer. Make and create new things. Think up new ideas. Lead the field. Think about fresh ways of doing things and different ways of delighting and helping people. Whatever your competitors do, you do something different. Keep monitoring what happens around you.

3. Track Your Profitability. *Your reputation will give you a good response rate, but your ROI (Return on Investment) is a better measure of the power of your reputation.* What income and wealth are you creating? Sure, people can say you're great, that they love you and that they endorse you, but it won't put food on your table. You'll sink a lot of energy and resources into generating your reputation. If you're just doing it for profile, then ROI is less relevant. But if you're doing it for profit, then what's coming back to you? If you're doing all of this for the recognition and attention, you must find ways to monitor the success or otherwise of your reputation. Set down measurable objectives. Find out what works, what doesn't and why. Then learn from the experience and build it into your strategy.

4. Overhaul Every Three to Six Years. *Where is the next trend, the next niche in your industry?* Think about a strong, personal overhaul of your reputation and your personal brand every few years. Perhaps your target market has been exploited enough and you need to move on to fresh pickings. Don't be scared to move on. Many millionaires have made and lost a fortune, only to do it again. You can do it again, and better, as you have all the lessons from the way you did it the first time!

5. Continue to Promote Yourself. *You need to be ubiquitous!* That's a posh word for 'everywhere'! In the right circles, of course. So work through a variety of different outlets. Great networker Will Kintish[36] taught me that the strategy for survival is visibility. The more your target audience hears your good name from many different sources, the more convinced they become of your value.

6. Monitor Your Competition. *Keep your friends close and your enemies closer still!* If a competitor is imitating you, look for the weaknesses in their position. There will be some, because if they are mimicking you, their reputation is not truly personal and won't stand up to scrutiny. All the work you have previously done will hopefully ensure that your reputation is built on solid ground.

7. Choose and Use Your Advocates. *Your resources are in your relationships.* You should identify key clients, customers and contacts, those who have come to know, like and trust you. Use them as your cheerleaders, your evangelists, your champions, your virtual sales force, your fans, your defenders and your word-of-mouth marketing arm. In many ways, you are not the best person to tell others how great you are. The best people for that role are the ones who are already using you. These are the ones who appreciate the difference you make and appreciate the value you offer.

8. Stay True to Your Vision, Your Goals and Your Core Values. *This is about getting what you want from work, business and life.* Purposeful reputation building gives you the confidence to market your value to the people that need you and that you want to work with you. Sometimes you can go such a long way down a certain road that you forget where you came from. People talk about staying grounded. Your character is what makes you who you are. But money, adulation and a myriad of opportunities can take your eye off the ball. You can sometimes lose sight of what you set out to be. So stay rooted in your character and stick to your task.

9. Stay Abreast of Industry Trends. *What's hot, what's new, what's now and what's next?* Make time, at least once every three months, to find out what the new consumer trends are, what your competitors are up to, the larger economic changes, technological developments – anything that might have an impact on your reputation and your expertise. As well as being a continuous learner, cultivate a network of your own experts and informants who can keep you up-to-date and current.

10. Protect Your Position. *Reputation marketing is as much about defending as developing.* Once you have established yourself as a leader in any way, shape or form, others will be keen to take your place. Look out for rivals and saboteurs! When you become good, people become jealous!

You're now on the right side of reputation management when it comes to being proactive and minimising damage. But what can you do if trouble occurs and you find your good name in a bad situation? Alternatively, what if, through your own mismanagement or misfortune, you have completely gone down a dead-end, or find yourself in the wrong lane and want to make the necessary changes or adjustments? *You have four key areas of redress:*

1. Change Your Target Audience. Expose your message to different people. You may have sufficiently worked and exploited one niche and are now ready to move on to another. You may have burned some bridges with a particular niche and need to start fresh. You may just want a fresh challenge. You can choose a similar target audience or a completely

265

different target audience. The choice is yours. Just do it on purpose.

2. Change Location. Move to a different town, vicinity, region or department. In short, 'get out of town! A fresh start in new surroundings may well do you the power of good. You can almost be who you want to be and start with a clean slate. At the very least, you can take the best elements from your old slate and carry them forward.

Nigel made a major career decision to end his position as a Baptist minister and move into the business world. After research into a number of franchise opportunities with his wife, he relocated the whole family to a completely different town. Without doubt, this was a courageous new start. Although he had some support structure, he had to build his network almost from the ground up. And the reputation he had built up in his previous role was of no use in his new role. Rather than make small changes in his current location, he opted for a clean break and the chance to be someone completely different in new surroundings.

3. Undergo Public Rehabilitation. This is the 'sticking plaster' approach where you rip off the old one and put on a new one. You stay right where you are and either slowly or quickly turn into somebody else. Time is a great healer, and people who adopt this approach are the kind who pick at the sticking plaster round the edges for days and weeks until the pain subsides! Others prefer the 'rip it off' method, which means enduring momentary agony, but then it's all over. Any kind of public apology, coming clean, resignation, demotion, swallowing of pride or show of remorse accompanies this way of repairing a reputation. It's akin to saying you got it wrong. This can result in big changes like a career move, smaller changes like a job or tiny changes like altering a minor personality defect.

 When I became a Christian, there were certain things I wanted to stop doing. There were other things I didn't want to stop doing, but they didn't go with the new territory! I used to swear and curse. I stopped. I used to steal. I stopped. I never used to listen. I started. It was painful at times but I did them overnight and got it out of the way in one go. And now I'm a much better man for it!

 In 'Artful Persuasion', author Harry Mills[37] tells the story of New York Mayor Ed Koch: "In 1980, Ed Koch appeared in one of those Sunday 'newsmaker' programmes in the aftermath of the city's financial crisis. Koch had spent $300,000 to put up bike lanes in Manhattan. As it turned out, cars were driving in the bike lanes, endangering the bikers.

"Meanwhile, some bikers were running over pedestrians because the pedestrians didn't know the bike lanes were there or didn't understand how they worked. It was a mess. The Mayor was coming up for re-election, and four or five journalists now had Koch cornered on this talk

show. *The whole purpose was to rip the Mayor's skin off for the bike lanes and for spending money foolishly when the city was nearly broke.*

"The trap was set. One reporter led off with, 'Mayor Koch, in light of the financial difficulties in New York City, how could you possibly justify wasting $300,000 on bike lanes?'

"Cut to Koch. Tight close-up. Everybody was expecting a half-hour disaster. Koch smiled and he said, 'You're right. It was a terrible idea.' He went on, 'I thought it would work. It didn't. It was one of the worst mistakes I ever made.' And he stopped.

"Now nobody knew what to do. They had another 26 minutes of the programme left. They all had prepared questions about the bike lanes, and so the next person feebly asked, 'But, Mayor Koch, how could you do this?' And Mayor Koch said, 'I already told you, it was stupid. I did a dumb thing. It didn't work.' And he stopped again. Now, there were 25 minutes left and nothing to ask him. It was brilliant."

4. **Keep a Low Profile**. Let time pass before re-emerging with a fresh, changed image. After losing their jobs, many people take time out to regroup before starting another job. Very few jump into a new job the moment they finish the old one. This in-between time gives people time to catch their

breath and think what they are about. If your reputation is going down the wrong road, it is not always easy to switch lanes. You may need to go back to the junction and park for a while before going down a different road. Depending on your finances and how a short sabbatical might look on your CV, consider laying low 'in-between empires'. Like the emerging butterfly from the pupa, you may just emerge stronger, more powerful and more beautiful afterwards!

> *"Change is inevitable; progress is optional."*
> **Ancient proverb**

Assuming damage has been done and you have to play a reactive game, the more effort you put into keeping your reputation the better. The consequences of a damaged reputation can be far-reaching. It is very difficult to regain a reputation once it has been damaged.

> *"It takes a lifetime to build a reputation, and only a short time to lose it all."*
> **Joseph Neubauer**, former CEO, Aramark Worldwide

In fact, depending on the reasons for the damage, it is sometimes impossible to regain a reputation once it is lost. Some people hold grudges; some people don't give second chances. *But you should do all in your power to repair the two forms of reputation damage – external and self-inflicted.*

External Damage

If you become aware of a problem a client has with you, or if you hear that a competitor has bad-mouthed you to others, you need to act quickly. You should do everything within your power to make things right - immediately. Just one disappointed or disaffected person can have a ripple effect - you don't want the rumour to spread. You need to kill it at inception. It's better to apologise first and ask questions later. Talk to the client, face-to-face if possible, and find out what you need to do to repair the damage.

> *"Without wood a fire goes out;*
> *without gossip a quarrel dies down."*
> **The Bible, Proverbs 26:20**

But how are you going to know that you've upset someone or not made a good impression? More often than not, things are said behind your back rather than to your face. Understanding the dynamics of first impressions is particularly important here. If you have succeeded in creating a great reputation, then 'your reputation precedes you' when you meet someone for the first time. It is crucial that your first meeting, contact on the phone or even your email does not fall below their expectations.

There is a positive side to this, in that you can exceed their expectations and so boost your reputation, but you must not do less than fulfil their current expectations. If you fall below this line, you might just ruin your chances of winning that person's approval or that prospect's custom or business. You might also increase the chances that they tell others of their impression or possible disappointment. This can potentially destroy your reputation at a stroke!

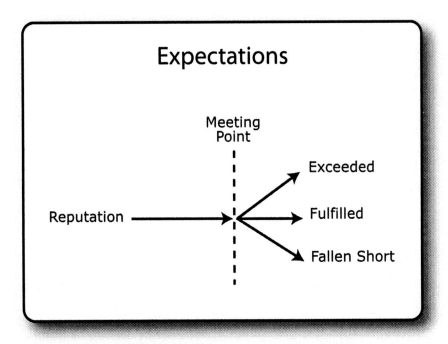

At the very least, you're looking to keep your esteem neutral. Not every interaction can be positive, just make sure you have no negative ones!

Self-inflicted Damage

The only problem with having a high reputation is that you must maintain your standards! If you have built yourself up – don't let carelessness bring you down. Your service must match up to your reputation. But sometimes it's not just the quality of your service that's the problem, but your integrity or morality.

You know how important it is that your reputation is authentic. It can't be based on falsehood. It must emanate from your inner character and qualities. The downside of this is that if you have consistent character flaws or serious moral difficulties, these will come to impact negatively on your reputation, however hard you try to conceal them. They could even destroy it.

If your reputation has been damaged by your own personality problems or if you know of something in you that has the potential to ruin your reputation, you must overcome that particular flaw. If you have great will power and self-control when you set your mind to something, you can succeed in changing these by yourself. But you may need help.

One of the best ways to make the necessary character and personality changes to enhance your reputation is through accountability. Being accountable means you need to be humble enough, or brave enough, to share your 'secret' with people who you trust. There's no room for ego in this.

> *"Ego management is an important first step in reputation management. When your ego is too big, it is impossible to best repair your reputation. Replace ego-driven communication with humble, honest and transparent communication and you will be on your way to repairing your reputation."*
> **Mike Paul**[38], reputation management expert known as 'The Reputation Doctor'

In fact, whether you are just building a reputation, want to maintain it or need to repair it, creating a strong accountability structure in your life can only pay dividends. Choose at least one person who can be your accountability partner. Your partner might be a close friend, your husband/wife or boyfriend/girlfriend, a parent or other relative, a spiritual adviser or church minister, or a therapist. They could be someone inside your business circle or industry. They could go under the guise of a friend or even a stranger who you share things with and run things past. Most people don't have one, so you will give yourself an advantage if you adopt this strategy. On a personal note, I have avoided making some crass errors in judgement by having accountability partners in my life!

Another avenue for accountability is with mentors or mastermind groups. These are key people who can speak into your life and help you see things you're too close to notice. Like a coach can read a football game better from the sidelines, having people whose opinions you accept and even admire 'on the outside' can keep you in line and help you move in the direction you want to.

Beware – real accountability demands full honesty. And it takes guts to share your struggles and failures. But the benefits for strengthening your character can be enormous. You need to give your accountability partner full permission to tell you off when they see you going down the wrong route, but encourage and praise you when you are making progress!

> *"An honest answer is like a kiss on the lips."*
> **The Bible, Proverbs 24:26**

So now you've seen how to go about proactively and reactively defending any damage to your reputation, whether self or externally inflicted. Now you need to consider general maintenance – how to evaluate and evolve your reputation over time.

Evaluating and Evolving Your Reputation
....

Maintaining your expertise is an ongoing process. If you persist, becoming a recognised expert can serve as your most effective marketing strategy. You can stay ahead of the game by keeping your personal reputation fresh. This is not a one-off process. Whatever your competitors do, you do something different. Keep monitoring what happens around you. You live in a rapidly changing world with many threats and opportunities.

Most professionals concentrate on the 'here and now' rather than taking some time to reflect on the impact of certain changes in their industry. They fail to see what trends are active. As a result, they get left behind and soon are perceived as out of touch. But not you. You will keep abreast of the marketplace, the players and the demands, so you're ready to move when you need to.

You must also be prepared to change your reputation. It can be done and sometimes it has to be done. Remember your reputation is simply how people respond to you in their thoughts, words and actions. You can't wholly control it, but you can give it your best shot.

If things go wrong or slip (which happens to almost everyone), then your reputation may take a hit. If people begin thinking the wrong things about you, you have two options. One, you can choose to live with it. This might be a valid option if the people in question are not your target audience. But if these are your kind

(cont'd on page 276)

The 22 Best Questions to Help You Evaluate Your Personal Reputation

1. Is your reputation really working?

2. What opportunities is it creating for you?

3. What revenue is it generating?

4. How well-known are you?

5. What influence do you have and with whom?

6. How easily can you change the feelings, actions and thoughts of those around you?

7. What leverage does your personal branding give you?

8. Is there a significant amount of goodwill in your name and reputation?

9. What is your status in your field?

10. Are you an icon - do you represent a concept that is larger than yourself?

11. What reach do you have - local, regional, national or global?

12. Are you any closer to making the board, nailing that pay increase, getting promoted, receiving that recognition you deserve?

13. Are there people copying or emulating you?

14. Are your competitors stretching ahead of you or struggling to keep up?

15. Is there any lack of awareness regarding who you are and what you do?

16. Is your reputation moving you forward?

17. How authentic is your reputation (who you want to be) when compared to your character (who you really are)?

18. How much do people like and trust you?

19. What's working with your reputation strategies, and what isn't?

20. What have been your biggest successes and failures in building your reputation?

21. What do you need to eliminate, stop doing or spend less time on to take your reputation to the next level?

22. What do you need to initiate, start doing or spend more time on to take your reputation to the next level?

of people and you are not influencing them in the right way, then you have to go to option two – you must be prepared to make changes.

Reputations naturally evolve, so what has taken you to where you are right now might not take you to where you need to be in two to three years' time. You must look for new and better ways to develop your reputation. The best way to do that is to ask yourself excellent, high quality evaluation questions. (See table on previous page.)

If you decide you want or need to make any changes, take a long view. Although change is often necessary, it is actually very difficult to change a reputation overnight. It is much easier to evolve your reputation over time.

Corporate Reputations

It is not the remit of this book on *personal reputations* to explore the whole gamut of *corporate reputations* and how to repair them. But whether you are employed or running your own company, your personal reputation can have a strong impact – negatively or positively – on the larger picture. Your personal credibility becomes entwined with any corporate image and reputation. This is a matter for concern – corporate reputation is having an increasing influence on the well-being of a company as a whole. If you work for yourself, your personal reputation is even more integral to your company's. You and the business are one. If you are an employee, keeping your own house in order is becoming more and more important. The consequences of not doing so can be more devastating for a company than ever before. We live in a world where there are people who are prepared to be malicious. And it's not just the journalists! It may be your competitors, either inside or outside your company. Leaks to the press and even personal blogs can be particularly damaging in this global information age.

> *"With each passing year, business success and sustainability become increasingly dependent on reputation. Media coverage of reputation alone has increased 108% over the past five years. As a topic of both conversation and debate, reputation now commands the attention of Web surfers and bloggers alike - nearly 187 million 'reputation' mentions surface when searching the Internet."*
> **Safeguarding Reputation™**, a wide-ranging 11-country survey on corporate reputation by global public relations firm Weber Shandwick, with KRC Research

The degree to which your personal name affects the company name depends on how well-known you are to the corporate world or the public. The higher profile you are, the more your company and you will be seen to be synonymous. Who can imagine Virgin without Sir Richard Branson, or Amstrad without Sir Alan Sugar? Their reputations certainly influence public perception of their companies.

You can focus a lot of your reputation building on actually building the name of your company rather than yourself. This may be beneficial if you are unsure of your ability to maintain your personal reputation. It also helps if you are growing a business to

277

sell, and you don't want your name too integrally associated with its success. Alternatively, in this world of journalistic intrusion, you may want to deflect attention from yourself so that you can live a more private existence.

"In today's world, where ideas are increasingly displacing the physical in the production of economic value, competition for reputation becomes a significant driving force, propelling our economy forward. Manufactured goods often can be evaluated before the completion of a transaction. Service providers, on the other hand, usually can offer only their reputations."
Alan Greenspan, American economist, Chairman of the Board of Governors of the US Federal Reserve from 1987 to 2006.

Reputation is increasingly a critical issue for businesses. So managing corporate reputations is a growing concern. It all boils down to trust. Does the consumer trust your brand, your company and yourself? Trust is difficult to control. To some degree, businesses are subject to the fickle whims of consumers. But this only increases the importance of being pro-active about a company's reputation. The messages you send out (your branding) is one way to influence your reputation.

Many companies actively seek to accumulate 'social capital' through good PR, which is sometimes completely disconnected from their actual products or services. The development of an emotional commitment to companies by their consumers is now a critical business success issue. Here are three ways companies aim to build up this kind of commitment, which is otherwise known as trust:

1. **Trust by Association.** Secure membership of your industry's professional organisations. Customers and clients are more likely to be reassured if they see the relevant logos and accreditation.

2. **Trust by Branding.** Does your brand stand for more than the product? Could it represent an ideal, a lifestyle or an aspiration that is attractive to the consumer? This is often done by giving added value, e.g. free, helpful information printed on products in addition to the product itself. This shows the company not only cares about selling the product but cares about the consumer too. For a long time, advertising has made much of identifying with lifestyle and aspirations rather than plugging the more mundane benefits of a product. Consumer perception is all-important.

3. **Trust by Ethics.** Do you invest in 'ethical capital'? Presenting your company as ethically trading or environmentally-friendly is a current trend that ties into current social values. The Co-op Bank, for example, has branded itself as an ethical bank, and Co-op supermarkets have been a leader in offering fairly-traded goods. 'Social responsibility' has become a buzzword because it is valued as a means of gaining customer goodwill and building reputation.

So, have a clear idea of how you want your company to be thought of, and ensure all your personal interactions and communications sing from the same hymn sheet.

Reputation Though Personal Branding

An indirect means of building your reputation is through your personal brand. I've outlined earlier the difference between reputation and brand (see Section 1). Here's a quick recap:

Your Personal Brand

What people see of you (the messages you put out and cues you give people)

Your Personal Reputation

What people think of you and say about you (how they respond to those messages and cues).

> "A brand is a reservoir of goodwill that
> takes a long time to build up."
> **David Haigh,** founder and chief executive of Brand Finance

If you want to begin building a personal brand in a way that maximises your reputation, here are the five key guidelines for success:

1. **Awareness.** *Keep your eyes open.* Make yourself aware of the changes in your business environment that may

affect your brand. This includes consumer trends, what your competitors are doing, legal changes, technological advances and shifts in the economy.

2. **Originality.** *Be unique.* This means meeting your client's needs in a way that is different from your competitors. You don't need to be radically different. Just different enough that people perceive the difference.

3. **Vision.** *Know where you're going.* You need a mission statement for your business and brand that is expressed in terms clear enough to map out a way forward. You and your team/company/business can then be inspired by it and guided by it.

4. **Futurisation.** *Build backwards from the reputation you want.* When creating a brand you need to first know what kind of reputation you are aiming for, and then make sure your brand is in line with that.

5. **Fluidity.** *Plan to evolve.* Don't have a static plan for your brand. You need to integrate learning and change into your plans. Ongoing assessment (finding out what's working and what isn't) and adapting is essential.

Branding has been through three key phases to arrive where it is today:

1. **Quality & Novelty = Aspirations.** Once it was about promoting a product or service through its quality or novelty. For example, a car advert might stress a bigger boot space, a faster acceleration, greater fuel economy or greater comfort. Then, to take a leap ahead of the competition instead of a small step, brands began to be promoted by developing an emotional connection with customers. This meant creating a resonance with them that is not based on function or quality but on aspirations or lifestyle. A product would be advertised by association. So, you might use celebrity endorsement, exotic locations, great music or humour – with adverts that say very little about the product itself. Brands have become more about perception than quality.

2. **Cynicism + Overload + Distrust.** More and more brands have competed for 'emotional space', and consumers have begun to see through this method. When the experience of a product fails to match up to the emotional promise of the advertising, they feel short-changed. For example, previous adverts may have shown a woman being chased by men after just one spray of a certain perfume. That was attempting a 'feel good' association of the perfume with an enviable lifestyle. But that idea has now worn thin – as women know that in reality a perfume is not going to change their life.

3. **Authenticity + Honesty + Connection.** Customers now abandon brands that seem to hold out a false hope or

promise, or promote an unattainable lifestyle. Phoniness is out – reality is in. So more and more brands are trying to connect with real life and real people. This resonates with reality rather than fantasy, meaning that, for example, you see 'real people' in adverts, or models that appear to be real people, rather than impossibly glamorous models. This makes it easier for people to believe in the brand and to identify with it.

Some advertisers have doubts about this, because it is possible that by using the *reality* route, you may lose the *aspirational* quality that excited customers about a brand in the first place. So, some brands have stuck with the aspirational method – but adapted it.

One way has been by doing adverts in a much more 'tongue-in-cheek' or ironic, humorous way. This tells the consumer that the advertiser is not trying to con them, by letting the consumer in on the joke. For example, Lynx deodorant is still promoted as making men more attractive, but the more recent adverts go completely over the top. A 2006 Lynx advert had thousands of bikini-clad women crawling out of the sea and running along the beach from miles around, just because one man had Lynx. It is obviously not meant to be taken seriously. But the underlying message that with Lynx you have a better chance with women is still there.

But once the emotional/aspirational route needs to become a joke in order to work, it shows that method is outmoded. The 'reality message' is the most progressive trend today for brands. From your own personal perspective, if your personal brand can deliver on its promises and create a true connection with people, there is a strong chance you will be successful.

Exploiting Your Reputation

....

Welcome to the wonderful world of fame, stardom, riches and celebrity! Exploiting your reputation becomes necessary when you either need to fast track your progress, mitigate some damage or leverage your good image for more of what you crave (attention, money or respect).

Once you achieve some kind of business celebrity status or rise to a certain level of salary, it may be possible to hire either a public relations (PR) manager or business agent. This can help you exploit your reputation financially, as well as maintain your image and secure you vital media coverage. You can exploit your personal reputation in two ways:

1. Commercial Exploitation. On a certain level, your reputation can secure you lucrative offers to speak, appear, endorse or champion. If you become a big name, you can use 'who you are' to make you more money. A PR agency can set up photoshoots, interviews, personal appearances and endorsement agreements for everything from crisps to aftershave! This kind of work can be especially lucrative if you have managed to secure a reputation through TV or radio appearances. Amstrad founder Sir Alan Sugar's TV series 'The Apprentice' has made him a household name. He could now probably earn more through adverts and endorsements than his own company, if he wished to go that route.

But beware – PR agents have a vested interest in pushing this type of brand exploitation to the limit. The more deals they cut for you, the more they earn. Are you prepared for the arduous regime that comes with the territory? Can you say 'no' to the endless round of appearances and 'opportunities' they create, if you need to? It may not suit your personality, family life, general lifestyle or business commitments. And you may want to keep your image associated only with quality products or services, so be discerning in what you agree to. You may have to hold a tight leash on your agent.

2. Career Exploitation. In the bigger companies, senior executives are now hiring representatives to act as career managers or advisers. Once you have a reputation, you can be headhunted. A business agent can act as your go-between and assess whether offers are a good move for you. They can also 'take you to market' in the right circumstances. They analyse your career and give career decision advice. Some will even take decisions for you. Highly-paid executives are prepared to pay for these services because their type of work means they don't have the time to do it themselves. And as executives don't want their employers to know they are considering a move, putting your job-hunting out to an agent means it's easier to keep your intentions confidential.

 Winchester-based Accipitor is a leading 'executive talent agency'. Managing Director Anthony McAlister says: "People come to us with very particular objectives. One, for example, has just been approached by a headhunter for an alternative role. He was unprepared for it and he wants to be brought up to speed in his interview technique. He wants to know what he's worth on the market before he progresses with this headhunter. On another assignment, we're working with a finance director in a FTSE-100 company. He has been passed over for the CEO role

where he is and he wants to know whether it's realistic for him to look for that outside his current organisation." ('Management Today', August 2005).

The Rules of Reputation Building and Keeping

There are certain rules you must obey if you are going to create the reputation you want and continue leveraging it for your long-term success. Good people come and go. Few have the energy, focus, diligence, persistence, integrity and courage to move from good to great.

These are the **17 Universal Laws of Reputation Building:**

1. Reputation Building is Not For the Complacent

You must realise that being good enough is no longer good enough. If you feel that your clients or customers will always be loyal, you will always rely on the reputation and good fortune that caused them to come to you in the first place. *This is yesterday's reputation.* What got you to where you are will not be enough to get you where you want to be in the next three to five years. Staying in your comfort zone shows a blatant ignorance of the **Ten Universal Laws of 21st Century Business**. There will come a time when you have to either have the courage of your convictions or go where the market tells you. You cannot do both and you cannot stay where you are.

2. Reputation Building is to be Envied

As you become more and more successful, people will start to copy you, mock you, steal from you and 'appropriate' your ideas, your methods and your intellectual property. Both emulation and ridicule acknowledge you as the leader in your field. Some will be jealous, some will be destructive. You must see that this is all part of being top of the pile.

3. Reputation Building is Authentic

It helps you if you don't copy others. Why? Because they're not you and you're not them. God made everyone different, unique and special. There is nobody else in the world with your blend of humour, experience, passions, expertise, qualities, skills, talents and knowledge. This is sometimes called *congruency* - your reputation must be congruent with your abilities. Trying to be someone you're not results at best in a fake and unsustainable image, and at worst a nervous breakdown. There is a difference between wanting someone else's reputation and being yourself. They don't go together. Sure, you can enhance your reputation (as you have seen) by getting around good people. But ultimately, *your reputation is yours to build.* Authenticity and congruency not only make it easier to define and establish your reputation, it makes you ultimately more attractive and credible. Don't copy others – be you and be yourself.

4. Reputation Building is Best Done Backwards

People rarely stumble on a great reputation. It doesn't usually happen by accident. They do it on purpose. And rather than starting at the beginning, they begin with the end in mind. *I call this 'futurising'!* Once you decide what you want to be known for, you have the blueprint for your reputation. And like a good architect works to good plans, you must then go about building that reputation. Decide what you want to create and then get to work. If your reputation is authentic and congruent with the person you really are, the people, the respect, the attention and the money will all come to you.

5. Reputation Building is Constant

The day you sit back and think you've done it all is the day the fire inside you goes out. Once you have built your reputation, you have to maintain it. So many reputations have been blown when people relax and let down their guard. *Lifelong employability is no longer guaranteed.* You must have a strong reputation to safeguard your position and give you options in an uncertain future. Your cluttered marketplace and your aggressive competitors mean you have to constantly be aware of who is doing what, where, when and how. In today's world of business, there is little time to rest. In brutal terms, there may be a bullet with your name on it that can make what you do obsolete. It could be a new idea, a new trend or a new competitor. You must stay alive to possibilities and keep your reputation alive and thriving. You must constantly solicit feedback, do more of what's working and do less of what isn't.

6. Reputation Building is Proactive

By evolving, you make yourself more difficult to copy and undermine. It is not enough to have a strong reputation, because others will follow. You must have a strong EVOLVING reputation. You must actively discern new directions, innovative processes, original ideas and new trends. You must stay ahead of the game. *Your reputation always has an impact.* It could be positive or negative, but it always has an impact. Develop the reputation you want for tomorrow. As you do that, today's reputation will take care of itself.

7. Reputation Building is Perception and Perception is Reality

It is not what you do and say, but how it is received and perceived that counts. You *can* control how others think of you *if you know what you are doing*. But do not be too carried away with great testimonials, referrals and endorsements. Fashions, trends and role models come and go with remarkable ease. What is 'in vogue' today may not hit the spot tomorrow. You reputation is to some extent a reactive game. You cannot please everyone all the time, and while you want to be liked and respected, this is not a popularity contest. You are in a reputation contest. The prizes are food on your table, money in your bank account, recognition of your achievements and satisfaction for your soul!

8. Reputation Building is Focused and Not Scattered

You must pick the right lane. In everything you say and do, ask yourself if it will get you closer to where you want to be in the minds of your target audience and ideal clients? Will it take you closer to or away from your ultimate reputation? You will never be all things to all people. Experts go deep and narrow, and that means one road. You can drive several cars, but they have to be on one road. As a personal example, I only speak on relationship and reputation marketing. That is, Turning Relationships Into Profits. In other words, I would say I am very, very strong on helping companies and individuals win more business through their reputation and relationships. I don't talk on presentation skills or negotiation or team building or leadership. There are better speakers and authors than me in those domains. But within my area of expertise, I drive three different cars – speaking, writing and consulting. Note that's not too many vehicles – just enough to be happy, effective and credible.

> *"Focusing obsessively on one niche, one feature and one market is almost always a better idea than trying to satisfy everyone. Compromise in marketing is almost always a bad idea. Extreme A could work. Extreme B could work. The average of A and B will almost never work."*
> **Seth Godin**, American author and speaker

9. Reputation Building is an Investment in Yourself

It's important you invest your time and your money back into your 'self-marketing'. You must keep on top of your learning and development and stay abreast of trends. You have to constantly take the temperature of your industry, ascertain the needs of your target market and track the activities of your rivals. *In some ways, you are the Chief Branding Officer of 'You Inc.'* Neglect your development at your peril. By attending seminars, courses and conferences, you invest time in good people. By studying good books and listening to powerful audio programmes, you invest time in a life-long education. Reputation building is much more of a long term relationship than a one-night stand!

> *"Read and learn. There are a million clues, case studies, books and proven tactics out there. You can't profitably ignore them until you know them, and you don't have the time or the money to make the same mistake someone*

else made last week. It's cheaper and faster to read about it than it is to do it."
Seth Godin, American author and speaker

10. Reputation Building is Not for the Faint Hearted

You need nerve to actively develop a certain reputation. It takes courage to be distinctive and plot your own course. You effectively have to tell the world what you, and you alone, can bring to the project, to the table, to the client or customer. If it was easy, everybody would be doing it. Writing a book isn't easy. Writing a series of articles takes effort and application. Asking for help isn't something that everyone feels comfortable with. Attending the right networking events and ploughing time and energy into key relationships takes a certain discipline and force of will. Not everyone can speak in public. That's why 5% of the world's population own 95% of the world's wealth. Successful people don't do much that is different to unsuccessful people. But very often the few different things that they do get their teeth into are the things that unsuccessful people don't or won't do. You may be isolated and ridiculed. You may be battered and bruised. But you'll be something rather than nothing, and you'll be amazed how lucky people think you are!

11. Reputation Building is an Abundant Activity

Having an abundance mentality means you don't blindly go about carving your reputation to the exclusion and expense of others. Everything you need in life, you have to go through other people to get. Your relationships are the source of your reputation, and therefore the source of your riches. Be a giver, who looks to help people, rather than a taker, who looks out for what he can get. To develop the reputation you desire, you will need help from others. And just as they help you, be ready to 'pay it forward'. That means that you don't necessarily have to pay it back to them; instead you should look to how you might help in growing their reputation. Remember your resources are in your relationships! Give and you will receive!

12. Reputation Building is an Energetic Activity

If you think you can build a reputation by standing on your head, speaking to one or two good audiences, turning out a nice book and writing one or two articles, you are right. If you think it will be a powerful one, then I'm not so sure. And if you think you can maintain your reputation with such minor development, my money says no! You will constantly have to be creative, to vociferously defend what you have so diligently built and to be vigilant for threats, dangers and complacency. You need energy, good health, sensible nutrition, rest and relaxation and *an appetite for the fight. Reputation building is a war that features a series of smaller battles.* Each one will drain you unless you stay topped up. Look after yourself and, hopefully, your reputation will look after you.

13. Reputation Building Won't Go Right First Time

This is a long-term game and a long-term gain. Your campaign will need revising, adjusting, reinventing or even scrapping. Don't be scared to say you've gone down the wrong path. Too many people have chased the wrong dream and worked too hard to fulfil the goals of others. Ensure it's what you really want rather than you pandering to any irrational or strongly held beliefs of people who are too close to you and want you to stay the same or go in a certain direction.

> *"I am tied to the stake, and I must stand the course."*
> **William Shakespeare**, great English playwright and poet
> (1564–1616), in 'King Lear', Act 3, Scene 7

14. Reputation Building Makes You Enemies

You're going to have to love it when people copy or mock you. Both emulation and ridicule acknowledge you as the leader in your field. Some people will be jealous of what you achieve. Some will be complimentary. Some will be destructive. It's all part of being top of the pile. The dictionaries define envy as a feeling of grudging admiration and desire to have something that is possessed by another. It is spite and resentment at seeing the success of another. What is the antidote? Have a thick skin to the people that envy, and a thin skin to the people that count. Keep evolving and you make yourself more difficult to copy and undermine.

> *"Jealousy is the tribute mediocrity pays to genius."*
> **Fulton J. Sheen**, pioneer of American
> religious broadcasting

15. Reputation Building Can Fail

Sometimes you'll get it wrong. Failure can be good, because if you're smart about the reflection, it teaches you where the benchmark is. There is no failure, only feedback. All of the world's most successful people have many significant failures behind them that have made them what they are. Valentino Rossi, eight-time world super bike champion, tells of how he moved up through the ranks, racing bigger and bigger bikes: "I allowed myself two years at each level. The first year I was always finding out where the limits were. There were a lot of crashes!"

16. Reputation Building Understands Group Influence

Remember the power of peer pressure in your school days? Well, it doesn't stop there. Adults can be and often are influenced by groups. If you want to build your reputation, you need to ensure that it is your influence in a group that wins out, not someone else's. If you have your own agenda that you have to win through on, don't cave in to peer pressure. Influence won't be gained by going along with the crowd, even if it is more convenient at the time. The crowd can be anonymous, so you need to stand out. You must be strong and confident if you are going to avoid being influenced, instead of influencing. Don't compromise!

> *"To thine own self be true."*
> **William Shakespeare,** great English playwright and poet
> (1564–1616) in 'Hamlet', Act 1, Scene 3

17. Reputation Building Can Be Celebrated!

Many people (myself included) are reticent about 'bigging themselves up' after big wins. Once a goal is achieved, the tendency is to say 'what's next?' You should celebrate your wins. Share your achievements with good people. You will have plenty of them!

"It feels good to be proud and even better to share it. Performance is emotional, and all things being equal, the difference is how you feel. The only question worth answering is how you plan, design and choose how you need to feel in order to do what you want to do. Celebrating helps you do that. It feels good to focus on the good stuff."
Andy Mouncey, Endurance Athlete
and Performance Coach

"A record is meaningless until it's shared."
Dame Ellen MacArthur, English sailor who broke the world record for the fastest solo circumnavigation of the globe in 2005

Leaving Your Legacy

As you come to the end of this reputational odyssey, the ultimate question beckons:

What legacy are you leaving behind?

You'll recall that *one of the ten benefits of building a strong reputation is an extended reach and influence.* How many lives are you touching? What lasting impressions are you making with people? Ultimately, what will people say about you when you are gone? What abiding memories will you leave people with? What will be your legacy?

This is the domain of *'future reputation building'* and helps you to decide what mark you will leave in your company, your family and your community at the end of your life.

When you're gone, you can no longer control your reputation. But Linda McCartney, the late wife of Paul and a famous vegetarian, still has a line of frozen foods at your local supermarket. Robert Ludlum, well-known deceased thriller writer, now has a new novel out. The Disney legacy lives on. Dale Carnegie's work lives on. Most of the professional services firms in the world still carry the names of long dead partners. Many retail giants like JC Penney have passed on, but their name lives on.

To conclude, before you picked up this book, you had two problems with your reputation:

296

1. **You didn't know exactly what your reputation was.**
2. **You didn't know exactly what you'd done to get it.**

Now you know exactly what a personal reputation is and also how important it can be. You should also appreciate exactly what yours is. In addition, you know how to design yours, how to build it, how to maintain it, how to extend it and how to defend it. You know you can achieve your goals and gain recognition and respect for what you do. You can be that 'go to' professional and the 'stand out choice' for what you do. You can become the obvious expert in a cluttered marketplace.

Your Reputation is the Reason Everyone Pays! Whether you want more RESPECT, ATTENTION OR MONEY, you can have it if you can build the necessary reputation. Whether you build it for PLEASURE, PROSPERITY OR POPULARITY, doing it on purpose will bring it within your grasp.

> *Do you want to turn an annual income*
> *into a monthly income?*
> *Do you want the phone to ring with people saying*
> *'you don't' know me but...'?*
> *Do you want to work less, make more and do*
> *the things you love doing?*

Many people have done these things, including myself. *It can take as little as 90 days to begin making the impact you truly want, if you do it on purpose!* So get excited, get started, get building and get enjoying a powerful, productive and prosperous personal reputation!

References

Section 1

....

1 Peter Thomson   www.peterthomson.com
                      'The UK's leading strategist on business and
                      personal growth'

2 Andy Gilbert   www.brainmagic.co.uk
                      'Developer of the critically acclaimed Go MAD
                      Thinking System'

3 Michael Gerber www.e-myth.com/pub/htdocs/aboutmeg.html
                      'Entrepreneur, author, speaker, revolutionary...'

4 Angus Matthew   www.poolonline.com/bios/bioamatthew.html
                      Relationship marketer

5 Lesley Everett www.lesleyeverett.com
                      'Europe's leading authority on personal
                      branding'

Section 2

....

6 Roger Hamilton www.rogerhamilton.com
                      'Asia's leading wealth consultant'

7 Penny Power   www.ecademy.com
                      Founder of Ecademy

8 Shay McConnon   www.shaymcconnon.com
                      Award-winning speaker and founder of People
                      First Ltd – 'an international Training and
                      Consultancy group'

9 Andy Mouncey www.coachco.co.uk

Inspirational performance coach

10 Nigel Risner www.nigelrisner.com

'One of Europe's leading key-note speakers and a powerful professional one-to-one coach to some of the world's leading business executives'

11 Jeffrey Gitomer www.gitomer.com

'A creative, on the edge, writer and speaker whose expertise on sales, customer loyalty, and personal development is world renowned'

12 Elsom and Mark Eldridge www.obvious-expert.com

Authors of 'How to Position Yourself As the Obvious Expert: Turbocharge Your Consulting or Coaching Business Now!'

13 Geoffrey Moore www.tcg-advisors.com

Managing Director at TCG Advisors and author of 'Dealing with Darwin: How Great Companies Innovate at Every Phase of Their Evolution'

Section 3

14 John Timperley www.puttick.com – see under 'clients'

'A consultant and former director with the world's largest professional services firm, PricewaterhouseCoopers'

15 Amanda Clarke www.optimum-training.com

Specialist in business and personal development coaching

16 Debra Searle   www.debrasearle.com

TV presenter, adventurer and motivational speaker

17 Michael Tipper   www.michaeltipper.com

Speaker and expert on improving creativity, enhancing memory and increasing reading speed

18 Clive Gott   www.clivegott.com

'Professional speaker, enter-trainer and author'

19 John C. Maxwell   www.maximumimpact.com

Leadership expert and best-selling author

20 Andy Cope   www.artofbrilliance.co.uk

'Professional trainer, qualified teacher, author and learning junkie'

21 Alison Jones   www.thepassiongroup.co.uk

Founder of The Passion Group which 'helps create inspired people, successful leaders, happy workforces and great company cultures'

22 Rajesh Setty   www.lifebeyondcode.com

Author, entrepreneur, chairman of CIGNEX Technologies and president of Foresight Plus, LLC

23 Rikki Arundel   www.professionalspeakers.org/cgi-bin/cgiwrap/psa/allegro.pl?RikkiArundel

Keynote speaker and coach 'helping people embrace the global gendershift'

24 Dan Poynter   www.parapublishing.com

Author, publisher and speaker

25 Andy Clark
www.speakers-academy.com
Trainer, motivational speaker and founder of the Speakers Academy

26 Nadio Granata
www.pngmarketing.co.uk
MD of Effective Events and LunchNet

27 Jay Abraham
www.abraham.com
Business performance expert and founder and CEO of Abraham Group, Los Angeles

28 John Sealey
www.yourmarketingmatters.co.uk
Business enhancement specialist and principal of Your Marketing Matters

29 Michael Heppell
www.michaelheppell.com
Business speaker and author of 'How to Be Brilliant'

30 Alan Stevens
www.mediacoach.co.uk
Director of Media Coach, which provides 'coaching and training in media skills and speaking skills'

31 Art Sobczak
www.businessbyphone.com
President of Business By Phone Inc., which 'specializes in working with business-to-business salespeople'

32 Harold Rose
www.mastertailoruk.com
MD of Master Tailor

33 Graham Jones
www.grahamjones.co.uk
Internet psychologist and Internet marketing speaker

34 Chris Cardell

www.cardellmedia.co.uk

'A world leader in Advanced Thinking and renowned for being able to show small and medium-sized businesses how to increase their profits'

35 Kate Broad

www.broadcomms.co.uk

Exceptional PR consultant

Section 4

• •

36 Mike Paul

www.mgppr.com

Strategic PR and reputation management counsellor and founder of MGP PR, 'a leading public relations firm' in New York

37 Will Kintish

www.kintish.co.uk

Business networking speaker and founder of Kintish – 'probably the best business networking trainers in the UK'

38 Harry Mills

www.millsonline.com

Mills Group CEO and expert on persuasion for the Harvard Manage Mentor Programme at Harvard Business School Publishing

Other Titles by Rob Brown

Do You Want to Turn Relationships into Repeat and Referral Business?

Are You Struggling With Networking?

Do You Want to Raise Your Profile and Reputation?

Rob's 'Business Bibles' can help, together with a range of **TRIP System®** relationship and reputation marketing resources and articles available at www.thetripsystem.com. Titles include:

Reputation Building Manual

An A4 workbook designed to help you put this book into practice! Packed with the full range of reputation building exercises, including worksheets, question banks, evaluation tools, supplementary information and recommended reading. See the resources section at www. thetripsystem.com for more details.

The Great Networking Questions Bible

Ever been stuck for what to say at a business event or social situation? Networking is simply talking and listening. It's building relationships. And if you want to network with people to Turn Relationships Into Profits, then here is your ultimate guide to all the questions and answers you will ever need!

The Liking Bible

Your pocket guide to more influence, better persuasion and deeper relationships. This unique collection of research on 'liking' and never-before-published scripts will get more people to like you more quickly. Now wouldn't that be useful in creating more business opportunities and furthering your career?

The Networking Bible

Your pocket guide to becoming a positive and productive networker. This punchy, powerful bible is packed with over 220 tips, ideas and scripts that you can use today to make the best use of your networking time, make better contacts and win more business!

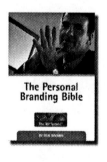

The Personal Branding Bible

Your pocket guide to a better reputation, greater positioning and increased business and career prospects. This powerful, hard-hitting bible contains over 150 of the best strategies, tips and tools that you can start on today to leverage your expert status and make people come to you for what you do.

The Referral Scripts Bible

Your pocket guide to the most powerful ways to ask for referrals. If you want to generate streams of high-quality referrals, buy this power-packed guide filled with loads of tips and actual scripts that you can use today to win more business!

The Remembering Names Bible

This is aimed at professionals who struggle with this most precious of skills - remembering names. If you can crack this skill, you will make more friends, influence more people, win more business, create more opportunities and find all kinds of social situations a lot more fun and productive!

The Trust Bible

Few things in life are more precious than trust. If you want to build credibility, reputation and trustworthiness, there are certain things you should be doing. This Bible reveals hundreds of tips, tools and strategies for building and winning trust with customers, clients, contacts and associates. An absolutely priceless investment in your relationships!

The Elevator Speech Bible

Almost every conversation you have with a stranger will contain the 'what do you do' question. Knowing how to answer it could mean the difference between mediocrity and success, struggling for business and winning all the business you need, creating opportunities and closing them. You need to know the common mistakes to avoid, the best possible ways to introduce yourself and how to move the conversation on. This Bible is your ultimate guide to answering this question with confidence, accuracy and potentiality!

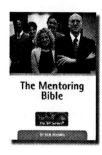

The Mentoring Bible

Talk to most of the world's successful people and you'll find that they've had guides, mentors, gurus, coaches and teachers to help them along the way. Mentoring is the most powerful way to fast-track your career, your ideas, your network and your knowledge. This Bible tells you how mentoring works, how to choose, approach and engage one, and how to make the relationship benefit both parties immeasurably!

The Ultimate Objection Handling Script Manual

Objections are generally a sign your prospect needs more convincing. There are brilliant and powerful ways to handle them, and aggressive, weak and negative ways to handle them. With close to 1,500 scripts and hundreds of tips and strategies for turning around any objection, this massive resource will be your ultimate guide to winning more sales, opening more closing doors and getting more people to say 'yes'!

About the Author

Rob Brown obtained an honours degree in Education from Leeds Metropolitan University in 1992, majoring in Physical Education and Mathematics. During his studies, and particularly after graduating in 1992, Rob indulged his love of travel, working for five years in American summer camps and travelling extensively throughout Australia, North America and South East Asia.

After graduating, Rob lived the expat life in Hong Kong from 1993-1997, working in teaching, journalism, advertising and even acting. A keen musician, he wrote and starred in two sell-out shows in the sister festival to Edinburgh, The Hong Kong Fringe, and brought out a successful album of jazz and pop songs which sold throughout the world!

After a sabbatical in the USA in 1996, where he became a Christian, Rob returned to the UK to work at the UK's 4th largest secondary school in his hometown of Hull in Yorkshire. He undertook a Masters in Human Resource Development in 1999, before being approached by worldwide health organisation, BUPA, for a direct sales position in private healthcare. This often brutal 'commission-only' role allowed Rob to cut his teeth selling and marketing, and gave him unique insight into what it takes to win business from scratch.

In 2002, he started work with a business networking company, the Kintish organisation, delivering network training. In 2004, he launched his own consultancy to help business professionals network more strategically, generate more high quality referrals and build more profitable client relationships.

In 2006, he invented and successfully trademarked the TRIP System®, which stands for Turning Relationships Into Profits. To fulfil the demand for his writing on relationship marketing, networking, referrals and reputation building, Rob launched a members-only website in 2006 - www.thetripsystem.com - to provide premium content articles, development programmes and educational materials to subscribers worldwide. He is a Fellow of the Professional Speaking Association and speaks internationally on relationship and reputation marketing for business professionals.

He lives in Nottingham with wife Amanda and daughters Georgia and Madison. When he's not speaking or writing, Rob juggles, plays chess and tennis, and enjoys cycling. His life mission is to give £1m to good godly causes in his lifetime!

Printed in the United Kingdom
by Lightning Source UK Ltd.
119094UK00001B/76-315